AMERICA IN THE 21ST CENTURY: POLITICAL AND ECONOMIC ISSUES

FEDERAL PROPOSALS FOR TAX REFORM

AMERICA IN THE 21ST CENTURY: POLITICAL AND ECONOMIC ISSUES

Additional books in this series can be found on Nova's website under the Series tab.

Additional E-books in this series can be found on Nova's website under the E-book tab.

ECONOMIC ISSUES, PROBLEMS AND PERSPECTIVES

Additional books in this series can be found on Nova's website under the Series tab.

Additional E-books in this series can be found on Nova's website under the E-book tab

AMERICA IN THE 21ST CENTURY: POLITICAL AND ECONOMIC ISSUES

FEDERAL PROPOSALS FOR TAX REFORM

STEVEN G. HANNAFORD
AND
EMILY WALLACE
EDITORS

NOVINKA

New York

Library of Congress Cataloging-in-Publication Data

ISBN: 978-1-62257-960-0

Published by Nova Science Publishers, Inc. † New York

CONTENTS

PREFACE

Chapter 1 – The President and leading Members of Congress have stated that fundamental tax reform is a major policy objective for the 112th Congress. Some Members have said that fundamental tax reform is needed in order to raise a large amount of additional revenue, which is necessary to reduce high forecast budget deficits and the sharply rising national debt. Congressional interest has been expressed in both a major overhaul of the U.S. tax system and the feasibility of levying a consumption tax. Some proponents of reform argue that the tax base should be broadened by reducing or eliminating many tax expenditures. An alternative to increasing tax revenues is cutting spending. Thus, Members are faced with considering the best mix of tax increases and spending cuts in order to reduce deficits and slow the growth of the national debt.

Proposals for fundamental reform have been made in reports by the National Commission on Fiscal Responsibility and Reform and the Debt Reduction Task Force of the Bipartisan Policy Center. In the 112th Congress, fundamental tax reforms are proposed in two companion bills, H.R. 25 and S. 13, *Fair Tax Act of 2011*; H.R. 99, *Fair and Simple Tax Act of 2011*; H.R. 1125, the *Debt Free America Act*; S. 727, the *Bipartisan Tax Fairness and Simplification Act of 2011*; H.R. 1040, the *Freedom Flat Tax Act*; and S. 820, the *Simplified Manageable, and Responsible Tax Act.* On April 13, 2011, President Obama presented his *Framework for Shared Prosperity and Shared Fiscal Responsibility*, which includes fundamental tax reform. On April 14, 2011, Representative Paul Ryan introduced H.Con.Res. 34, FY2012 budget resolution, which includes fundamental changes in the U.S. tax system. On March 20, 2012, House Budget Committee Chairman Paul Ryan released the committee's Fiscal Year 2013 Budget Resolution, *The Path to Prosperity: A*

Blueprint for American Renewal. An evaluation of these proposals would consider the effects on equity, efficiency, and simplicity.

A temporary individual AMT patch for 2010 and 2011 was included in the *Tax Relief, Unemployment Insurance Authorization, and Job Creation Act of 2010*, which became P.L. 111- 312 on December 17, 2010. The patch increased the individual AMT exemption amounts. Some proponents of tax reform argue that the AMT should be repealed or a permanent patch should be passed. The repeal or passage of a permanent patch of the individual AMT would require a major increase in taxes to offset the large revenue loss.

Options for reforming the corporate income tax are under consideration. The concept of lowering the marginal corporate income tax rate and broadening the corporate income tax base has been advocated by some Members of Congress. Other options for reform include corporate tax integration and the replacement of the income tax system with a consumption tax.

The current system of U.S. taxation of international business is complex and difficult to administer. Furthermore, critics argue that the current system is not sufficiently neutral, which results in economic inefficiency. Proposals to reform the system include the replacement of the current hybrid system with either a territorial tax system or a residence-based system.

Chapter 2 – The Obama Administration released the President's FY2012 budget proposal on February 14, 2011. According to the Administration's estimates, the tax proposals in the budget would increase revenues $280 billion over the next 10 years. The Administration's estimates were made relative to a current policy budget baseline, which assumes certain polices that are scheduled to change in the future by law will not. In contrast, the Congressional Budget Office (CBO) and Joint Committee on Taxation (JCT) make their projections relative to a current law budget baseline, which assumes future policy changes will occur as prescribed by current laws.

This difference in baselines may result in the Administration's estimates being different than future CBO and JCT estimates.

This chapter provides a broad overview of the provisions included in the President's budget request. The budget groups proposed tax provisions into several general categories. The Administration estimates the net budgetary impact of the proposals in each category as follows:

- Tax cuts for families and individuals would reduce revenues by $92.0 billion over 5 years and $253.6 billion over 10 years.

- Tax cuts for business would reduce revenues by $46.6 billion over 5 years and $116.4 billion over 10 years.
- Tax incentives to promote regional growth would reduce revenues by $4.7 billion over 5 years and $5.3 billion over 10 years.
- Extending certain expiring tax provisions through 2012 would reduce revenues by $21.7 billion over 5 years and 22.3 billion over 10 years.
- Reducing certain tax expenditures to pay for three years of AMT relief would increase revenues by $113.9 billion over 5 years and $321.3 billion over 10 years.
- Other revenue changes and provisions the proposal terms loophole closers would increase revenues by $166.2 billion over 5 years and $356.5 billion over 10 years.

Congress has begun its consideration of the President's budget. The House and Senate Budget Committees are responsible for formulating and reporting an annual budget resolution. The budget committees typically develop the budget resolution as they receive information and testimony from various sources, such as the Administration, CBO, and congressional committees with jurisdiction over spending and revenues. The timetable established in the Congressional Budget Act directs the Senate Budget Committee to report a budget resolution by April 1 and for the House and Senate to reach final agreement on a budget resolution by April 15.

Chapter 3 – America's system of business taxation is in need of reform. The United States has a relatively narrow corporate tax base compared to other countries—a tax base reduced by loopholes, tax expenditures, and tax planning. This is combined with a statutory corporate tax rate that will soon be the highest among advanced countries. As a result of this combination of a relatively narrow tax base and a high statutory tax rate, the U.S. tax system is uncompetitive and inefficient. The system distorts choices such as where to produce, what to invest in, how to finance a business, and what business form to use. And it does too little to encourage job creation and investment in the United States while allowing firms to benefit from incentives to locate production and shift profits overseas. The system is also too complicated—especially for America's small businesses. For these reasons, the President is committed to reform that will support the competitiveness of American businesses—large and small—and increase incentives to invest and hire in the United States by lowering rates, cutting tax expenditures, and reducing complexity, while being fiscally responsible. This chapter presents the President's Framework for business tax reform. In laying out this Framework, the President recognizes that tax reform will take time, require work on a bipartisan basis, and benefit from additional feedback from stakeholders and experts. To start that process, this chapter outlines what the President believes should be five key elements of business tax reform.

Chapter 4 – Many of the provisions of the Economic Growth and Tax Relief Reconciliation Act of 2001 (EGTRRA; P.L. 107-16) and the Jobs Growth Tax Relief Reconciliation Act of 2003 (JGTRRA; P.L. 108-27), henceforth referred to as the Bush tax cuts, are scheduled to expire at the end of 2012. Two bills introduced in the Senate—S. 3412, the Middle Class Tax Cut Act, offered by Senator Reid and S. 3413, the Tax Hike Prevention Act, offered by Senator Hatch—propose to extend some or all of these tax cuts for one year through the end of 2013. A bill introduced in the House—H.R. 8, the Job Protection and Recession Prevention Act of 2012—is virtually identical to S. 3413 except for its treatment of a business expensing provision. Media reports indicate that votes on these proposals are expected to occur before the August 2012 recess.

This chapter is organized to first provide an overview of the Bush tax cuts, followed by brief summaries of S. 3412 and S. 3413, henceforth referred to as the Reid and Hatch proposals, respectively. Revenue loss estimates of certain provisions of these bills are also included, as well as a brief summary of H.R. 8. In addition, detailed summary tables comparing the Reid and Hatch proposals—to each other and to current law—are provided. Finally, this chapter concludes with a brief overview of the current policy debate surrounding the partial or full extension of the Bush tax cuts.

In: Federal Proposals for Tax Reform
Editors: S. G. Hannaford, E. Wallace
ISBN: 978-1-62257-960-0

Chapter 1

TAX REFORM: AN OVERVIEW OF PROPOSALS IN THE 112TH CONGRESS*

James M. Bickley

SUMMARY

The President and leading Members of Congress have stated that fundamental tax reform is a major policy objective for the 112th Congress. Some Members have said that fundamental tax reform is needed in order to raise a large amount of additional revenue, which is necessary to reduce high forecast budget deficits and the sharply rising national debt. Congressional interest has been expressed in both a major overhaul of the U.S. tax system and the feasibility of levying a consumption tax. Some proponents of reform argue that the tax base should be broadened by reducing or eliminating many tax expenditures. An alternative to increasing tax revenues is cutting spending. Thus, Members are faced with considering the best mix of tax increases and spending cuts in order to reduce deficits and slow the growth of the national debt.

Proposals for fundamental reform have been made in reports by the National Commission on Fiscal Responsibility and Reform and the Debt Reduction Task Force of the Bipartisan Policy Center. In the 112th Congress, fundamental tax reforms are proposed in two companion bills, H.R. 25 and S. 13, *Fair Tax Act of 2011*; H.R. 99, *Fair and Simple Tax*

---

* This is an edited, reformatted and augmented version of Congressional Research Service, Publication No. R41591, dated May 31, 2012.

Act of 2011; H.R. 1125, the *Debt Free America Act*; S. 727, the *Bipartisan Tax Fairness and Simplification Act of 2011*; H.R. 1040, the *Freedom Flat Tax Act*; and S. 820, the *Simplified Manageable, and Responsible Tax Act.* On April 13, 2011, President Obama presented his *Framework for Shared Prosperity and Shared Fiscal Responsibility*, which includes fundamental tax reform. On April 14, 2011, Representative Paul Ryan introduced H.Con.Res. 34, FY2012 budget resolution, which includes fundamental changes in the U.S. tax system. On March 20, 2012, House Budget Committee Chairman Paul Ryan released the committee's Fiscal Year 2013 Budget Resolution, *The Path to Prosperity: A Blueprint for American Renewal.* An evaluation of these proposals would consider the effects on equity, efficiency, and simplicity.

A temporary individual AMT patch for 2010 and 2011 was included in the *Tax Relief, Unemployment Insurance Authorization, and Job Creation Act of 2010*, which became P.L. 111- 312 on December 17, 2010. The patch increased the individual AMT exemption amounts. Some proponents of tax reform argue that the AMT should be repealed or a permanent patch should be passed. The repeal or passage of a permanent patch of the individual AMT would require a major increase in taxes to offset the large revenue loss.

Options for reforming the corporate income tax are under consideration. The concept of lowering the marginal corporate income tax rate and broadening the corporate income tax base has been advocated by some Members of Congress. Other options for reform include corporate tax integration and the replacement of the income tax system with a consumption tax.

The current system of U.S. taxation of international business is complex and difficult to administer. Furthermore, critics argue that the current system is not sufficiently neutral, which results in economic inefficiency. Proposals to reform the system include the replacement of the current hybrid system with either a territorial tax system or a residence-based system.

INTRODUCTION

The President and leading Members of Congress have stated that fundamental tax reform is a major policy objective for the 112th Congress. Some Members have said that fundamental tax reform is needed in order to raise a large amount of additional revenue, which is necessary to reduce high forecast budget deficits and the sharply rising national debt. Other Members maintain that a revenue increase is unnecessary because spending reductions can be sufficient to reduce the deficit.[1] Congressional interest has been expressed in both a major overhaul of the U.S. tax system and the feasibility of levying a consumption tax over the existing tax system.[2] Some proponents of reform argue that the tax base should be broadened by reducing or eliminating many tax expenditures. "Tax expenditures are revenue losses resulting from federal tax provisions that grant special tax relief designed to encourage certain kinds of behavior by taxpayers or to aid taxpayers in special circumstances."[3] If tax expenditures are reduced substantially or a consumption tax is levied or both, then the marginal income tax rates could be reduced. An alternative to increasing tax revenues is cutting spending. Thus, Members are faced with considering the best mix of tax increases and spending cuts in order to reduce deficits and slow the growth of the national debt.

In December 2010, The National Commission on Fiscal Responsibility and Reform (the "Commission") issued a report titled *The Moment of Truth*, which proposed extensive broadening of both the individual income tax base and the corporate income tax base by eliminating all business tax expenditures and almost all individual tax expenditures.[4] Marginal individual and corporate income tax rates would be reduced, and the individual alternative minimum tax would be abolished. The taxation of foreign-source income would be changed by moving to a territorial system.[5] On November 17, 2010, the Debt Reduction Task Force of the Bipartisan Policy Center issued a report titled *Restoring America's Future*.[6] This report also recommended that individual and corporate income tax bases be broadened by reducing or eliminating most tax expenditures. Marginal individual and corporate income tax rates would be lowered, and the individual alternative minimum tax would be eliminated. In addition, this report recommended that a 6.5% value-added tax be levied. The recommendations of these two reports may influence the tax reform debate in the 112th Congress.

In the 112th Congress, Members of Congress have introduced numerous bills containing incremental or marginal adjustments in the tax code in an attempt to redistribute income, reallocate resources, change individual behavior, etc. Proposed incremental or small tax adjustments are considered tax changes.[7] In contrast, fundamental tax reform concerns a major proposed overhaul of the U.S. tax system, which affects the entire tax system or a major component of the system.

In the 112th Congress, bills proposing fundamental tax reform have been introduced. Two companion bills, H.R. 25 (introduced by Representative Rob Woodall) and S. 13 (introduced by Senator Saxby Chambliss), *Fair Tax Act of 2011*, would replace the individual income tax, the corporate income tax, all payroll taxes, the self-employment tax, and the estate and gift taxes with a 23% (tax-inclusive) national retail sales tax. Representative David Dreier introduced H.R. 99, *Fair and Simple Tax Act of 2011*, which would establish an alternative determination of tax liability for individuals. Representative Michael Burgess introduced H.R. 1040, *Freedom Flat Tax Act*, which would authorize an individual or a person engaged in business activity to make an irrevocable election to be subject to a flat tax (in lieu of the existing tax provisions). Representative Chaka Fattah introduced H.R. 1125, *Debt Free America Act*, which would impose a transaction fee of 1% on the entire amount of specified intermediate and final transactions. Revenue raised from this fee would be sufficient to eliminate the national debt during a 10-year period and phase out the income tax on individuals. Senator Richard C. Shelby introduced S. 820, the *Simplified, Manageable, and Responsible Tax Act*, which was modeled after the flat tax proposal formulated in 1981 by Hall and Rabushka and would levy a consumption tax as a replacement for individual and corporate income taxes and estate and gift taxes. This proposal would have two components: a wage tax and a cash-flow tax on businesses. On April 14, 2011, House Budget Committee Chairman Representative Paul Ryan introduced H.Con.Res. 34, which includes major tax reforms. On April 15, 2011, the House passed this FY2012 budget resolution, which includes fundamental changes in the U.S. tax system.[8] On March 20, 2012, House Budget Committee Chairman Paul Ryan released the committee's Fiscal Year 2013 Budget Resolution, *The Path to Prosperity: A Blueprint for American Renewal*. This resolution includes fundamental tax reform.

Three major fiscal reform proposals containing major tax reforms have been introduced or updated during 2011 and 2012. On April 13, 2011, President Obama presented his *Framework for Shared Prosperity and Shared Fiscal Responsibility*, which proposes to reduce the deficit by $4 trillion over 12 years or less. The President's plan includes comprehensive tax reform. On June 29, 2011, the President's Fiscal Commission published updated estimates of its proposal.[9] On February 13, 2012, President Obama released his FY2013 budget that included major changes in taxes.

This chapter primarily covers fundamental tax reform because CRS reports are available concerning the other three categories of tax reform: tax reform based on the elimination of the individual alternative minimum tax (AMT), proposals for reforming the corporate income tax, and proposals for reforming the U.S. taxation of international business.[10]

FUNDAMENTAL TAX REFORM OPTIONS

Two broad fundamental tax reform categories for addressing the severe deficit problem are base-broadening and levying a new tax. Some of the revenue from base-broadening and a new tax could be used to reduce marginal tax rates.

Base-Broadening

Some Members of Congress have expressed concern about the large number and high cost of tax expenditures.[11] Examples of tax expenditures are the deduction for mortgage interest on owner-occupied residences and the deduction for property taxes on owner-occupied residences. Many of these tax expenditures are seen as targets to be reduced or eliminated. Congress may want to consider whether the benefits of a particular tax expenditure exceed the costs of that tax expenditure.[12] Arguably, the current tax reform debate deals with broadening the individual and corporate income tax bases and lowering marginal tax rates.

New Tax

Revenue from a new tax would allow the retention of more tax expenditures and lower reductions in other tax expenditures. Furthermore, revenue from a new tax could finance a larger reduction in marginal income tax rates and permit a smaller reduction in federal spending. Broad categories have received the most attention: consumption and environmental taxes.

Broad-Based Consumption Tax

In recent Congresses, three major types of broad-based consumption taxes have been included in congressional tax proposals: the value-added tax (VAT), the retail sales tax, and the flat tax. These possible broad-based consumption taxes have the potential of a robust revenue yield.

Value-Added Tax

A value-added tax is a tax on the value that a firm adds to a product at each stage of production.[13] The value the firm adds is the difference between a firm's sales and a firm's purchases of inputs from other firms. The VAT is collected by each firm at every stage of production.

There are three alternative methods of calculating VAT: the credit method, the subtraction method, and the addition method. Under the credit method, the firm calculates the VAT to be remitted to the government by a two-step process. First, the firm multiplies its taxable sales by the tax rate to calculate VAT collected on sales. Second, the firm credits VAT paid on inputs against VAT collected on sales and remits this difference to the government. The firm calculates its VAT liability before setting its prices to fully shift the VAT to the buyer. Under the credit-invoice method, a type of credit method, the firm is required to show VAT separately on all sales invoices and to calculate the VAT credit on inputs by adding all VAT shown on purchase invoices.

Under the subtraction method, the firm calculates its value added by subtracting its cost of taxed inputs from its sales. Next, the firm determines its VAT liability by multiplying its value added by the VAT rate. Under the addition method, the firm calculates its value added by adding all payments for untaxed inputs (e.g., wages and profits). Next, the firm multiplies its value added by the VAT rate to calculate VAT to be remitted to the government.

All developed nations, except Japan, use the credit-invoice method. Japan uses the subtraction method.

Retail Sales Tax

A retail sales tax is a consumption tax levied only at a single stage of production, the retail stage. The retailer collects a specific percentage markup in the retail price of a good or service, which is then remitted to the government.[14] As of February 1, 2010, the Tax Foundation reports that 45 states had retail sales taxes.[15]

Flat Tax

A flat tax could be levied based on the proposal formulated by Robert E. Hall and Alvin Rabushka of the Hoover Institution.16 Their proposal would have two components: a wage tax and a cash-flow tax on businesses. (A wage tax is a tax only on salaries and wages: a cash-flow tax is generally a tax on gross receipts minus all outlays.) It is essentially a modified VAT, with wages and pensions subtracted from the VAT base and taxed at the individual level. Under a standard VAT, a firm would not subtract its wage and pension contributions when calculating its tax base. Under the flat tax, some wage income would not be included in the tax base because of exemptions. Under a standard VAT, all wage income would be included in the tax base.

Environmental Tax

Environmental taxes have been proposed to reduce pollution and raise revenue. The most frequently discussed energy tax is a *carbon tax* that would be levied on the volume of carbon emitted.[17] This tax is frequently recommended by economists, but the Obama Administration is attempting to implement a cap and trade system. Another alternative energy tax would be higher *gasoline taxes*.[18]

FRAMEWORK OF EVALUATION

In evaluating any change in tax policy, the prevailing framework is to analyze the tax policy for equity, efficiency, and simplicity. Tradeoffs may exist between these three objectives. For example, if greater income equality is desired, this may conflict with the goal of economic efficiency.

Equity

Economic theory maintains that it is not possible to make interpersonal comparisons of utility. Hence, whether a change in the distribution of income, with gainers and losers, is an improvement in the national welfare is a value judgment. The effects on different groups, however, can be measured and debated. Thus, the following questions can be examined.

How will different income groups be affected annually and over their lifetimes? Will taxpayers in similar circumstances pay approximately the same amount of taxes? What will be the effect on taxpayers in different age groups? Will there be distributional effects by region of the country? How will minority groups be affected? What will be the tax incidence on families versus single taxpayers?

Efficiency

Tax policy should promote economic efficiency; that is, a tax change should be as neutral as possible by minimizing economic distortions.[19] Low marginal tax rates tend to lessen distortions.

Many efficiency questions concern household decisions. What will be the effect of a tax change on households' decisions to save versus consume? Will households' choices of leisure versus work be affected? Will household decisions about the composition of goods and services consumed be affected?

Other efficiency questions concern firms' decisions. What will be the effect on firms' decisions concerning the method of financing (debt or equity), choice among inputs, type of business organization (corporation, partnership, of sole proprietorship), and composition of output?

Simplicity

The greater the simplicity of the tax system, the lower will be the administrative and compliance costs. Thus, tax policy should eliminate any unnecessary complexity and promote transparency.

Numerous questions concerning simplicity arise; among them are the following: How will a tax change affect federal administrative costs? Will the administrative costs of state and local governments change? How will compliance costs of households be affected? Will business compliance costs change?

Other Tax Reform Issues

Alternative Minimum Tax for Individuals

In 1969, Congress enacted the individual alternative minimum tax (AMT) to make sure that everyone paid at least a minimum of income taxes and still preserve the economic and social incentives in the tax code. The combined effects of inflation and the legislative reductions in the regular income tax have expanded the number of taxpayers subject to the AMT. Consequently, Congress has passed temporary increases in the basic exemption for the AMT to limit the number of taxpayers subject to the AMT. Most recently, an AMT patch for 2010 and 2011 was included in the *Tax Relief, Unemployment Insurance Authorization, and Job Creation Act of 2010*, which became P.L. 111-312 on December 17, 2010. Some proponents of tax reform argue that the AMT should be repealed or a permanent patch should be passed, but either reform would require a major increase in taxes to offset the large revenue loss.[20]

Business Taxation

Federal taxes on business income have differential effects.[21] For example, non-corporate income is taxed less than corporate income, debt financing is an expense but equity financing is not, and depreciation rules favor machines and equipment over structures and inventory. These differential effects distort investment decisions, lessen economic efficiency, and lower economic welfare. Several options have been proposed to reform federal business taxation.[22]

First, comprehensive taxation of corporate income and lower tax rates would eliminate or reduce most major distortions. In the 112th Congress, the concept of lowering the marginal corporate income tax rate and broadening the corporate income tax base has been advocated by some Members of Congress.

Second, corporate tax integration would eliminate the double taxation of corporate income by altering the general system of taxing corporate-source income. Integration could apply to both retained earnings and dividends and thus all corporate profits ("full integration"), or the treatment only of earnings that are distributed ("partial integration").

Third, a broad-based consumption tax could be levied that would replace individual and corporate income taxes.

International Taxation

The rapid growth of the foreign trade sector in the U.S. economy and the expansion of international flows of capital have increased the importance of appropriate U.S. international tax practices.[23] The two alternative principles on which countries can base their international tax systems are residence and territory.

Under a residence system, a country taxes its own residents (or domestically chartered "resident" corporations) on their worldwide income, regardless of its geographic source. Under a territorial system, a country taxes only income that is earned within its own borders. Currently, the United States has a hybrid system with elements of both a residence system and a territorial system. The United States taxes both income of foreign firms earned within its borders as well as the worldwide income of its U.S.-chartered firms. U.S. taxes, however, do not apply to the foreign income of U.S.-owned corporations chartered abroad. A U.S. firm can indefinitely defer U.S. tax on its foreign income if it conducts its foreign operations through a foreign-chartered subsidiary corporation; U.S. taxes do not apply as long as the foreign subsidiary's income is reinvested overseas. With some exceptions, U.S. taxes apply only when the income is remitted to the U.S.- resident parent as dividends or other intra-firm payments. While the United States taxes worldwide income on either a current or deferred basis, it also allows a foreign tax credit for foreign taxes paid on a dollar-for-dollar basis against U.S. taxes in order to avoid the double-taxation of income.[24]

The current system is complex and difficult to administer. Furthermore, critics argue that the current system is not sufficiently neutral, which results in economic inefficiency. The system provides a tax incentive to invest in countries with low tax rates and a disincentive to invest in countries with high tax rates. Proposals to reform the U.S. international tax system include the replacement of the current hybrid system with either a territorial tax system or a residence-based system.[25]

FUNDAMENTAL TAX REFORM LEGISLATION IN THE 112TH CONGRESS

In the 112th Congress, several bills for fundamental tax reform have been introduced.

Representative David Dreier's Proposal

H.R. 99. The *Fair and Simple Tax Act of 2011* was introduced on January 5, 2011, and referred to the House Ways and Means Committee. This bill would establish an alternative determination of tax liability for individuals. A "simplified taxable income" would be taxed at the rates of 10% on the first $40,000, 15% on the income over $40,000 but under $150,000, and 30% on the income over $150,000. Simplified taxable income would equal gross income less the sum of deductions for personal exemptions, the deduction allowed for the acquisition of indebtedness with respect to the principal residence, the deduction allowed for state and local income taxes, the deduction allowed for charitable giving, and the deduction allowed for medical expenses. The estate and gift taxes would be repealed. The alternative minimum tax exemption amounts would be indexed for inflation. The maximum corporate income tax rate would be reduced to 25%. The 15% rate on dividends and capital gains of individuals would be reduced to 10%. The basis for assets for purposes of determining capital gain or loss would be indexed for inflation. This bill would create tax-free accounts for retirement savings, lifetime savings, and lifetime skills. Examples of qualified life skills include assessments of skill levels, development of an individual employment plan, career planning, occupational skills training, on-the-job training, and entrepreneurial training. This bill would repeal the adjusted gross income threshold in the medical care deduction for individuals under age 65 who have no employer health coverage. This bill would make the research credit permanent. This bill would repeal Title LX of the Economic Growth and Tax Relief Reconciliation Act of 2001 (EGTRRA) relating to sunset of provisions. This bill would repeal Section 107 of the Jobs and Growth Tax Relief Reconciliation Act of 2003 relating to application of EGTRRA sunset to this title.

Representative Rob Woodall/Senator Saxby Chambliss Proposal

H.R. 25

The *Fair Tax Act of 2011* was introduced on January 5, 2011, by Representative Rob Woodall and referred to the Committee on Ways and Means. A companion bill, **S. 13**, the *Fair Tax Act of 2011,* was introduced on January 25, 2011, by Senator Saxby Chambliss and referred to the Senate Finance Committee.

This proposal would repeal the individual income tax, the corporate income tax, all payroll taxes, the self-employment tax, and the estate and gift taxes and levy a 23% (tax-inclusive) national retail sales tax as a replacement. The tax-inclusive retail sales tax would equal 23% of the sum of the sales price of an item and the amount of the retail sales tax.

Every family would receive a rebate of the sales tax on spending amounts up to the federal poverty level (plus an extra amount to prevent any marriage penalty). The Social Security Administration would provide a monthly sales tax rebate to registered qualified families. The 23% national retail sales would not be levied on exports. The sales tax would be separately stated and charged. Social Security and Medicare benefits would remain the same with payroll tax revenue replaced by some of the revenue from the retail sales tax. States could elect to collect the national retail sales tax on behalf of the federal government in exchange for a fee.

Taxpayer rights provisions are incorporated into the act. The sales tax would sunset at the end of a seven-year period beginning on the enactment of this act if the Sixteenth Amendment is not repealed. This amendment provided Congress with the "power to lay and collect taxes on incomes.... "

Representative Chaka Fattah's Proposal

H.R. 1125

The *Debt Free America Act* was introduced on March 16, 2011, and referred to the Committee on Ways and Means and three other committees. This act states that its purposes are to raise sufficient revenue from a fee on transactions to (1) eliminate the national debt within 10 years and phase out the individual income tax, and (2) provide incentives for private sector investment in capital goods, clean energy generation, and infrastructure development.

This act would amend the Internal Revenue Code to impose a transaction fee of 1%, offset by a corresponding nonrefundable income tax credit, on every specialized transaction that uses a payment instrument, including any check, cash, credit card, transfer of stock, bonds, or other financial instrument. This act defines "specified transaction" to (1) exclude any deposit into a personal account of an individual and any transfer between accounts, and (2) include retail and wholesale sales, purchases of intermediate goods, and financial and intangible transactions.

The fees would be collected by the seller or financial institution servicing the transaction and would be paid to the U.S. Treasury. This act would establish in the legislative branch the Bipartisan Task Force for Responsible Fiscal Action, which would review the fiscal imbalance of the federal government, identify factors affecting the long-term fiscal imbalance, analyze potential courses of action, and provide recommendations and legislative language to improve the long-term fiscal imbalance.

This act would repeal after 2021 the individual income tax, refundable and nonrefundable personal tax credits, and the alternative minimum tax (AMT) on individuals.

This act would direct the Secretary of the Treasury to (1) prioritize the repayment of the national debt to protect the fiscal stability of the United States; and (2) study and report to Congress on the implementation of this act.

Senator Ron Wyden's Proposal

S. 727

The *Bipartisan Tax Fairness and Simplification Act of 2011* was introduced on April 5, 2011, and referred to the Senate Finance Committee. This act was also sponsored by Senator Dan Coats and is often referred to as the Wyden-Coats proposal. This proposal would reform the current income tax base rather than changing to a consumption base. This bill has three stated purposes: (1) to make the federal individual income tax system simpler, fairer, and more transparent; (2) to make the federal corporate income tax rate a flat 24%, repeal the corporate alternative minimum tax, and eliminate special tax preferences that favor particular types of businesses or activities; and (3) to partially offset the federal budget deficit through the increased fiscal responsibility resulting from these reforms.

The progressive individual income tax would have three rates: 15%, 25%, and 35%. The individual alternative minimum tax would be eliminated. The standard deduction would almost triple. While most deductions would be eliminated, the bill would include deductions for mortgage interest and charitable contributions. The bill would permanently extend the enhancements of the child tax credit, the earned income tax credit, and the dependent care credit. The bill would consolidate the three existing types of IRAs into a new retirement savings account, and a new lifetime savings account. A married couple would be able to contribute up to $14,000 per year to tax-favored retirement and savings accounts. The corporate tax rate would be 24% of taxable income.

The corporate tax base would be broadened by the elimination of numerous tax credits, deductions, and exclusions from income. The growth of small businesses would be encouraged by allowing businesses with gross annual receipts of up to $1 million to permanently expense all equipment and inventory costs in a single year. The bill includes numerous provisions to improve tax compliance.

Representative Michael C. Burgess's Proposal

H.R. 1040

The **Freedom Flat Tax Act** was introduced on March 11, 2011, by Representative Burgess and referred to the House Committee on Ways and Means and the House Committee on Rules.

This proposal would authorize an individual or a person engaged in business activity to make an irrevocable election to be subject to a flat tax (in lieu of the existing tax provisions). The flat tax was based on the concepts of the Hall-Rabushka flat tax proposal. This act would also repeal estate and gift taxes.

For individuals not engaged in business activity who select the flat tax, their initial tax rate would be 19%, but after two years this rate would decline to 17%. The individual flat tax would be levied on all wages, retirement distributions, and unemployment compensation. An individual's taxable income would also include the taxable income of each dependent child who has not attained age 14 as of the close of such taxable year.

The flat tax would have "standard deductions" that would equal the sum of the "basic standard deduction" and the "additional standard deduction."

The "basic standard deduction" would depend on filing status:

- $30,320 for a married couple filing jointly or a surviving spouse
- $19,350 for a single head of household
- $15,160 for a single person or a married person filing a separate return

The "additional standard deduction" would be an amount equal to $6,530 for each dependent of the taxpayer. All deductions would be indexed for inflation using the consumer price index (CPI).

For individuals engaged in business activity who select the flat tax, their initial tax rate would be 19% (declining to 17% when the tax was fully phased in two years after enactment) on the difference between the gross revenue of the business and the sum of its purchases from other firms, wage payments, and pension contributions.

For those employees electing the flat tax, government employers and employers of nonprofit organizations would pay a flat tax on their employees' fringe benefits, except retirement contributions, because activities of government entities and tax-exempt organizations would be exempt from the business tax.

Any congressional action that raises the flat tax rate or reduces the amount of the standard deduction would require a three-fifths (supermajority) vote in both the Senate and the House of Representatives. The effective date of the flat tax would be calendar year 2012.

Senator Richard C. Shelby's Proposal

S. 820

The **Simplified, Manageable, and Responsible Tax Act** was introduced on April 14, 2011, and referred to the Senate Finance Committee. This act is modeled after the flat tax proposal formulated in 1981 by Hall and Rabushka and would levy a consumption tax as a replacement for individual and corporate income taxes and estate and gift taxes. This proposal has two components: a wage tax and a cash-flow tax on businesses.

The individual wage tax would be levied at a 17% rate. The individual wage tax would be levied on all wages, salaries, pension distributions, and unemployment compensation. An individual's taxable income would include taxable income of each dependent child who has not attained age 14 as of the close of the taxable year. The individual wage tax would not be levied on Social Security receipts. Thus, the current partial taxation of Social Security payments to high-income households would be repealed. Social Security contributions would continue to be taxed; that is, they would not be deductible and would be made from after-tax income. Firms would pay the business tax on their Social Security contributions. Individuals would pay the wage tax on their Social Security contributions. The individual wage tax would have "standard deductions" that would equal the sum of the "basic standard deduction" and the "additional standard deduction."

The "basic standard deduction" would depend on filing status. For tax year 2012, the basic standard deduction would have been the following:

- $26,810 for a married couple filing jointly or a surviving spouse
- $17,120 for a single head of household
- $13,410 for a single person
- $13,410 for a married person filing a separate return

The "additional standard deduction" would be an amount equal to $5,780 for each dependent of the taxpayer. All deductions would be indexed for inflation using the consumer price index (CPI).

Businesses would pay a tax of 17% on the difference (if positive) between gross revenue and the sum of purchases from other firms, wage payments, and pension contributions. This business tax would cover corporations, partnerships, and sole proprietorships. Pension contributions would be deductible but there would be no deductions for fringe benefits. State and local taxes (including income taxes) and payroll taxes would not be deductible.

If the business's aggregate deductions exceed gross revenue, then the excess of aggregate deductions can be carried forward to the next year and increased by a percentage equal to the three-month Treasury rate for the last month of the taxable year.

Government employers and employers of nonprofit organizations would pay a 17% tax on their employees' fringe benefits, except retirement contributions, because activities of government entities and tax-exempt organizations would be exempt from the business tax.

This bill would be effective for taxable years beginning after December 31, 2011. A supermajority of three-fifths of the Members of the House or Senate would be required to (1) increase any federal income tax rate; (2) create any additional federal income tax rate; (3) reduce the standard deduction; or (4) provide any exclusion, deduction, credit, or other benefit which results in a reduction in federal revenues.

OTHER LEGISLATION IN THE 112TH CONGRESS RELEVANT TO FUNDAMENTAL TAX REFORM

H.R. 462. (Sponsor: Representative Bob Goodlatte)

The *Tax Code Termination Act* was introduced on January 26, 2011, and referred to the House Committee on Ways and Means. After December 31, 2015, this bill proposes to terminate the tax code except for self-employment taxes, Federal Insurance Contributions Act taxes, and Railroad Retirement taxes. This proposal declares that any new federal tax system should be a simple and fair system that (1) applies a low rate to all Americans, (2) provides tax relief for working Americans, (3) protects the rights of taxpayers and reduces tax collection abuses, (4) eliminates the bias against savings and investment, (5) promotes economic growth and job creation, and (6) does not penalize marriage or families. This bill would require that the new federal tax system be approved by Congress not later than July 4, 2015.

H.Con.Res. 34. (Sponsor: Representative Paul Ryan)

House Budget Chairman Paul Ryan introduced this continuing resolution on April 14, 2011, "establishing the budget for the United States Government for fiscal year 2012 and setting forth appropriate budgetary levels for fiscal years 2013 through 2021." On April 15, 2011, this bill was passed by the House. This FY2012 budget resolution proposes to reduce future deficits and slow the growth of the national debt. Major reforms in the tax system are proposed. The summary regarding taxes states that the budget resolution

- keeps taxes low so the economy can grow, eliminates roughly $800 billion in tax increases imposed by the President's health care law, and prevents the $1.5 trillion tax increase called for in the President's budget; and
- calls for a simpler, less burdensome tax code for households and small businesses, lowers tax rates for individuals, businesses, and families, sets top rates for individuals and businesses at 25%, and improves incentives for growth, savings, and investment.[26]

Fiscal Year 2013 House Budget Resolution

On March 20, 2012, the House Budget Committee Chairman Paul Ryan released the committee's Fiscal Year 2013 Budget Resolution, *The Path to Prosperity: A Blueprint for American Renewal*.[27] In contrasting the vision of this budget resolution with the President's budget, the House Budget Committee states that their "Path to Prosperity" has the following budgetary effects:[28]

- **Spending:** Cuts spending by $5 trillion relative to President's budget.
- **Taxes:** Prevents President's tax increases; reforms broken tax code to make it simple, fair, and competitive; clears out special interest loopholes and lowers everybody's tax rates to promote growth.
- **Deficits:** Brings deficits below 3% of GDP by 2015; reduces deficits by over $3 trillion relative to President's budget; puts budget on path to balance.
- **Debt:** Reduces debt as a share of the economy over the next decade; charts a sustainable trajectory by reforming the drivers of the debt; pays off the debt overtime.
- **Size of Government:** Brings size of government to 20% of economy by 2015, allowing the private sector to grow and create jobs.
- **National Security:** Prioritizes national security be preventing deep, indiscriminate cuts to defense; identifies strategy-driven savings,

while funding defense at levels that keep America safe by providing $554 billion for the next fiscal year for national defense spending.

- **Health Security:** Repeals President's health care law; advances bipartisan solutions that take power away from government bureaucrats and puts patients in control; no disruption for those in or near retirement; Ensures a strengthened Medicare program for future generations, and with less support given to the wealthy and more assistance for the poor and the sick.

In discussing its "Pro-Growth Tax Reform" the House Budget Committee makes the following key points:[29]

- The tax code has become a broken maze of complexity and political favoritism, overgrown with special-interest loopholes and high marginal rates that stifle economic growth and job creation.
- This budget reforms the broken tax code to spur job creation and economic opportunity by lowering rates, closing loopholes, and putting hardworking taxpayers ahead of special interests. The pro-growth reforms ensure the tax code is fair, simple, and competitive.
- This budget consolidates the current six individual income tax brackets into just two low brackets of 10% and 25% and repeals the Alternative Minimum Tax.
- This budget reduces the corporate rate to 25% and shifts from a "worldwide" system of taxation to a "territorial" tax system that puts American companies and their workers on a level playing field with foreign competitors.
- This budget rejects the President's call to raise taxes. Instead, it broadens the tax base to maintain revenue growth at a level consistent with current tax policy and at a share of the economy consistent with historical norms of 18% to 19% in the following decades.

Other Major Fiscal Reform Proposals

Three major fiscal reform proposals containing broad tax reforms were introduced or updated during the second session of the 112th Congress. On April 13, 2011, President Obama presented his *Framework for Shared Prosperity and Shared Fiscal Responsibility*, which proposes to reduce the deficit by $4 trillion over 12 years or less. The President's plan includes comprehensive tax reform. On June 29, 2011, the President's Fiscal Commission published updated estimates of its proposal. On February 13, 2012, President Obama released his budget for FY2013, which included proposals for major tax changes.

President Obama's April 2011 Fiscal Reform Proposal

On April 13, 2011, President Obama gave a speech in which he presented his *Framework for Shared Prosperity and Shared Fiscal Responsibility*. The President set a goal of reducing the deficit by $4 trillion in 12 years or less.[30] Under tax reform, the fact sheet for his proposal states

> The President is calling on Congress to undertake comprehensive tax reform that produces a system which is fairer, has fewer loopholes, less complexity, and is not rigged in favor of those who can afford lawyers and accountants to game it.
>
> He believes we cannot afford to make our deficit problem worse by extending the Bush tax cuts for the wealthiest Americans.
>
> He also supports efforts to build on the Fiscal Commission's goal of reducing tax expenditures so that there is enough savings to both lower rates and lower the deficit. Reform should be designed to ask more of those who can afford it while protecting the middle class and promoting economic growth.
>
> In addition, as he explained in the State of the Union, the President is continuing his effort to reform our outdated corporate tax code to enhance our economic competitiveness and encourage investment in the United States. By eliminating loopholes, reducing distortions and leveling the playing field in our corporate tax code, we can use the savings to lower the corporate tax rate for the first time in 25 years without adding to the deficit.[31]

President's Fiscal Commission Updated Estimates

On June 29, 2011, the President's Fiscal Commission published updated estimates of its proposal.32 Under the Fiscal Commission's plan, deficits were projected to decline as follows: 8.1% of GDP in 2011, 6.4% of GDP in 2012, 2.3% of GDP in 2015, and 1.2% of GDP in 2020.33 Under the Fiscal Commission's updated estimates, deficits are projected to fall from 9.3% of

GDP in 2011, 6.8% of GDP in 2012, 2.6% of GDP in 2015, and 1.8% of GDP in 2020.34 The Fiscal Commission's explanation is:

> The deficit ... numbers differ from original estimates in the Commission report largely because the increased debt burden created by the 2010 tax cut deal and, more significantly, because of lower economic growth assumptions which have significantly pushed down revenue projections.[35]

The Commission's updated estimates also cover changes in the levels of spending, revenues, and debt.

President Obama's FY2013 Budget Proposals

On February 13, 2012, President Obama released his FY2013 budget, which proposed numerous changes in tax law. "If enacted, those changes would reduce revenues by $61 billion in 2012 and by $2.4 trillion ... during the 2013-2022 period relative to the amounts in CBO's baseline."[36]

The Congressional Budget Office describes these proposed revenue changes as[37]

- Extending and Modifying the 2001 and 2003 Tax Reductions

> Various income tax provisions that were originally enacted in EGTRRA [*Economic Growth and Tax Relief Reconciliation Act of 2011*] and JGTRRA [*Jobs and Growth Tax Relief Reconciliation Act of 2003*], modified by the American Recovery and Reinvestment Act of 2009 (ARRA, P.L. 111-5) and extended by the 2010 tax act are scheduled to expire at the end of December 2012.
>
> ... the President has called for permanently extending, at 2012 levels, the tax rates on income, capital gains, and dividends for couples with income below $250,000 who file joint tax returns and for single filers with income below $200,000. (Both of those income thresholds would be adjusted for inflation since 2009.) For taxpayers with income above the thresholds, the President proposes to maintain the income tax rates, the phaseout of the personal exemption, and the limit on itemized deductions that are scheduled to take effect in January 2013 under current law and to tax capital gains at a rate of 20 percent. In addition, the President proposes to continue the $1,000 child tax credit (which was raised by $500 in EGTRRA) and the reduced earnings threshold at which families can qualify for at least some of that credit (which was enacted in ARRA).

- Providing Relief from the Alternative Minimum Tax

...the President proposes to reduce the number of taxpayers who would be subject to the AMT by permanently setting various parameters of the tax at the levels that were in effect in calendar year 2011 and indexing those amounts for inflation in later years.

- Limiting Deductions and Exclusions

The president proposes to limit the extent to which higher-income taxpayers can reduce their tax liability through certain deductions and exclusions to 28 percent of those deductions and exclusions.

- Modifying Estate and Gift Taxes

The President's budget calls for setting the parameters of the estate, gift, and generation-skipping transfer taxes at the levels that were in effect during calendar year 2009, starting in January 2013. Under that proposal, the amount of an estate that would effectively be exempt from the estate tax would be set permanently at $3.5 million (and at $7 million per couple in most cases); any amount above that effective exemption level would be taxed at a rate of 45 percent.

- Other Revenue Proposals

[Other] proposals include a set of changes to the U.S. system of taxing international income.... The changes include targeting specific sources of tax avoidance associated with intangible assets (such as patents and trademarks) and modifying tax rules for calculating foreign tax credits and expenses related to foreign operations. The tax credit for research and experimentation expired at the end of calendar year 2011. The President proposes to permanently reinstate it, in modified form, and make it retroactive to January 1, 2012. The American Opportunity Tax Credit, which was created by ARRA and extended through December 2012 by the 2010 tax act, provides an annual tax credit of up to $2,500 per student for qualifying postsecondary education expenses. The President also proposes to make that credit permanent and to index the amount of qualifying expenses and the phaseout limits for inflation. The Build America Bonds program, which was also created by ARRA, provides subsidy payments to state and local governments that equal 35 percent of their interest costs on taxable bonds issued through December 31, 2010, to finance capital expenditures. The program has expired for bonds issued after that date; the President proposes to permanently reinstate and expand it but to lower the subsidy rate to 30 percent through 2013 and to 28 percent thereafter. The President also proposes to extend through 2012 a provision that allows all firms that invest in equipment to deduct the full costs of that equipment from their taxable income immediately, instead of spreading the costs out over time. Other proposals that CBO and JCT estimate would increase revenues include repealing the "last-in, first-out" method of accounting for inventories; imposing a "financial crisis responsibility fee"; providing short-term tax relief to employers and expanding the base for the payroll tax for unemployment compensation; and boosting spending for enforcement activities of the Internal Revenue Service.

FEASIBILITY OF TAX REFORM IN 2012

Public finance experts and policymakers differ in their views of the feasibility of major tax reform in 2012. On May 15, 2012, House Speaker John A. Boehner said that "before the November elections, the House would vote on a package that will include extension of the 2001 and 2003 tax cuts and will set up a process for broad tax reform."[38] On May 11, 2012, a committee aide said that "House Ways and Means Committee staff is preparing legislation for both a one-year extension of the 2001 and 2003 tax cuts and comprehensive tax reform in case lawmakers want to bring a reform bill to the floor during the lame-duck session...."[39] On May 8, 2012, Mark Mazur, Treasury deputy assistant secretary for tax analysis, said at a Senate Finance Committee hearing that "despite offering a framework for corporate tax reform earlier in the year, the administration has no plan to release a comprehensive [corporate] tax reform proposal soon."[40]

End Notes

[1] Americans for Tax Reform (ATR) opposes all tax increases as a matter of principle. In the 112th Congress, 236 U.S. Representatives and 41 U.S. Senators have taken an ATR pledge never to raise income taxes, http://www.atr.org, May 30, 2012.

[2] For more information, see CRS Report R41641, *Reducing the Budget Deficit: Tax Policy Options*, by Molly F. Sherlock.

[3] Senate Committee on the Budget, *Tax Expenditures: Compendium of Background Material on Individual* Provisions, Washington: GPO, December 2008, p. 2.

[4] The National Commission on Fiscal Responsibility and Reform, *The Moment of Truth*, December 2010, 65 p.

[5] Ibid., p. 33.

[6] The Debt Reduction Task Force, Bipartisan Policy Center, *Restoring America's Future*, November 17, 2010, 138 p.

[7] Some of these proposed tax changes are examined in CRS reports.

[8] House Committee on the Budget, Chairman Paul Ryan, *The Path to Prosperity, Fiscal Year 2012 Budget Resolution*, 63 p.

[9] National Commission on Fiscal Responsible and Reform, *Updated Estimates of the Fiscal Commission Proposal*, June 29, 2011, 14 p.

[10] Citations of these CRS reports are shown in footnotes in the sections covering these other categories of tax reform.

[11] For an analysis of tax expenditures, see CRS Report RL34622, *Tax Expenditures and the Federal Budget*, by Thomas L. Hungerford.

[12] For background material on tax expenditures, see Senate Committee on the Budget, *Tax Expenditures: Compendium of Background Material on Individual Provisions*, S. Prt. 111-58, 111th Congress, 2nd Sess., December 2010, 983 p.

[13] For a comprehensive overview of the concept of a U.S. VAT, see CRS Report R41602, *Should the United States Levy a Value-Added Tax for Deficit Reduction?*, by James M. Bickley. For a primer on the VAT, see CRS Report R41708, *Value-Added Tax (VAT) as a Revenue Option: A Primer*, by James M. Bickley.

[14] For a contrast between the VAT and the national sales tax, see CRS Report RL33438, *A Value-Added Tax Contrasted With a National Sales Tax*, by James M. Bickley.

[15] *State Sales, Gasoline, Cigarette, and Alcohol Tax Rates by State, 2000-2010*, Tax Foundation. Available at http://www.taxfoundation.org, April 18, 2011.

[16] For a comprehensive analysis of the flat tax, see CRS Report 98-529, *Flat Tax: An Overview of the Hall-Rabushka Proposal*, by James M. Bickley.

[17] For an analysis of the carbon tax, see CRS Report R40242, *Carbon Tax and Greenhouse Gas Control: Options and Considerations for Congress*, by Jonathan L. Ramseur and Larry Parker.

[18] For an analysis of the gasoline tax, see CRS Report R40808, *The Role of Federal Gasoline Excise Taxes in Public Policy*, by Robert Pirog.

[19] The loss in economic efficiency due to a tax is referred to by economists as the deadweight loss or excess burden of the tax.

[20] For an examination of the alternative minimum tax for individuals, see CRS Report RL30149, *The Alternative Minimum Tax for Individuals*, by Steven Maguire.

[21] For an overview of the reform of federal business taxation, see CRS Report RL33171, *Federal Business Taxation: The Current System, Its Effects, and Options for Reform*, by Donald J. Marples. For an overview of corporate tax reform issues, see CRS Report RL34229, *Corporate Tax Reform: Issues for Congress*, by Jane G. Gravelle and Thomas L. Hungerford.

[22] For a comprehensive analysis of these options, see CRS Report RL33171, *Federal Business Taxation: The Current System, Its Effects, and Options for Reform*, by Donald J. Marples.

[23] This section of this report summarizes some basic concepts in CRS Report RL34115, *Reform of U.S. International Taxation: Alternatives*, by Jane G. Gravelle. Some excerpts are stated from this report. For a primer on international corporate taxation, see CRS Report R41852, *U.S. International Corporate Taxation: Basic Concepts and Policy Issues*, by Mark P. Keightley.

[24] Ibid., p. 2.

[25] Ibid., pp. 12-16.

[26] House Committee on the Budget, Chairman Paul Ryan, *The Path to Prosperity*, April 5, 2011, p. 5.

[27] House Budget Committee, Chairman Paul Ryan, *The Path to Prosperity: A Blueprint for American Renewal*, Fiscal Year 2013 Budget Resolution, March 20, 2012, 98 p.

[28] Ibid., p. 5.

[29] Ibid., p. 57.

[30] The White House, Office of the Press Secretary, *Fact Sheet: The President's Framework for Shared Prosperity and Shared Fiscal Responsibility*, April 13, 2011, p. 1.

[31] Ibid., p. 5.

[32] National Commission on Fiscal Responsible and Reform, *Updated Estimates of the Fiscal Commission Proposal*, June 29, 2011, 14 p.

[33] Ibid., p. 4.

[34] Ibid.

[35] Ibid.

[36] Congressional Budget Office, *An Analysis of the President's 2013 Budget*, March 2012, p. 6.

[37] Ibid., pp. 7, 10.

[38] Michael Beller, "House Will Vote on Bush Tax Cuts, Framework for Tax Reform Before Election, Boehner Says," *Tax Notes Today,* May 16, 2012.

[39] Brett Ferguson and Rachel Boehm, "House Aides Preparing for Possibility of Tax Reform Bill in Lame-Duck Session," *Daily Tax Report*, May 14, 2012, p. G9.

[40] Meg Shreve, "No White House Tax Reform Plan Coming Soon, Treasury Nominee Says," *Tax Notes Today*, May 9, 2012.

In: Federal Proposals for Tax Reform
Editors: S. G. Hannaford, E. Wallace
ISBN: 978-1-62257-960-0

Chapter 2

AN OVERVIEW OF MAJOR TAX PROPOSALS IN THE PRESIDENT'S FY2012 BUDGET*

Mark P. Keightley, James M. Bickley, Gary Guenther, Thomas L. Hungerford, Steven Maguire, Donald J. Marples and Molly F. Sherlock

SUMMARY

The Obama Administration released the President's FY2012 budget proposal on February 14, 2011. According to the Administration's estimates, the tax proposals in the budget would increase revenues $280 billion over the next 10 years. The Administration's estimates were made relative to a current policy budget baseline, which assumes certain polices that are scheduled to change in the future by law will not. In contrast, the Congressional Budget Office (CBO) and Joint Committee on Taxation (JCT) make their projections relative to a current law budget baseline, which assumes future policy changes will occur as prescribed by current laws.

This difference in baselines may result in the Administration's estimates being different than future CBO and JCT estimates.

---

* This is an edited, reformatted and augmented version of Congressional Research Service, Publication No. R41699, dated May 4, 2012.

This chapter provides a broad overview of the provisions included in the President's budget request. The budget groups proposed tax provisions into several general categories. The Administration estimates the net budgetary impact of the proposals in each category as follows:

- Tax cuts for families and individuals would reduce revenues by $92.0 billion over 5 years and $253.6 billion over 10 years.
- Tax cuts for business would reduce revenues by $46.6 billion over 5 years and $116.4 billion over 10 years.
- Tax incentives to promote regional growth would reduce revenues by $4.7 billion over 5 years and $5.3 billion over 10 years.
- Extending certain expiring tax provisions through 2012 would reduce revenues by $21.7 billion over 5 years and 22.3 billion over 10 years.
- Reducing certain tax expenditures to pay for three years of AMT relief would increase revenues by $113.9 billion over 5 years and $321.3 billion over 10 years.
- Other revenue changes and provisions the proposal terms loophole closers would increase revenues by $166.2 billion over 5 years and $356.5 billion over 10 years.

Congress has begun its consideration of the President's budget. The House and Senate Budget Committees are responsible for formulating and reporting an annual budget resolution. The budget committees typically develop the budget resolution as they receive information and testimony from various sources, such as the Administration, CBO, and congressional committees with jurisdiction over spending and revenues. The timetable established in the Congressional Budget Act directs the Senate Budget Committee to report a budget resolution by April 1 and for the House and Senate to reach final agreement on a budget resolution by April 15.

INTRODUCTION

On February 14 , 2011, the Administration released the President's FY2012 budget proposal.[1]

This chapter provides a broad overview of the proposed tax provisions in the budget. Also provided are the Administration's 5- and 10-year revenue estimates for individual tax proposal line-items.[2]

Tax Cuts for Families and Individuals

The tax cuts for individuals and families that are proposed in the President's budget would expand and extend certain middle-income tax relief while allowing tax cuts for upper-income taxpayers to expire. Overall, the Administration estimates that the proposed tax cuts for families and individuals would reduce revenues by $92.0 billion over 5 years and $253.6 billion over 10 years.

Expand Earned Income Tax Credit

Beginning in 2013, the President's budget would make permanent the expansion in eligibility for the Earned Income Tax Credit (EITC) that was originally part of the American Recovery and Reinvestment Act of 2009 (ARRA; P.L. 111-5). For tax years 2009 and 2010, ARRA increased the maximum credit amount from $4,824 to $5,657 for working families with three or more children. This translated into an increase in the maximum credit rate for this group of families from 40% to 45%. The Tax Relief, Unemployment Insurance Reauthorization, and Job Creation Act of 2010 (P.L. 111-312) extended the ARRA modifications through 2012.[3]

Expand Child and Dependent Care Tax Credit

Taxpayers may currently claim a nonrefundable tax credit to partially offset child and dependent care expenses. The credit is equal to 35% of up to $3,000 of eligible expenses for one child or dependent, and up to $6,000 of eligible expenses for more than one child. The credit rate decreases by one percentage point for every $2,000 of adjusted gross income (AGI) over $15,000 until the percentage of expenses for which it may be claimed reaches 20% (at incomes above $43,000).

The President's budget proposes to increase the income level at which the credit rate begins to decrease from $15,000 to $75,000 beginning in 2012. Under the President's proposal the 35% credit rate would decrease by one percentage point for every $2,000 of AGI over $75,000 until the credit rate reached 20% (at incomes above $103,000).

Automatic Enrollment in IRAs, Employer Enrollment Tax Credit, and Small Employer Plan Tax Credit

The President's budget proposes to require employers (except those with fewer than 10 employees and those in business for less than two years) who do not currently offer a retirement plan to offer automatic enrollment in an IRA to all employees beginning in 2013.[4] The employee automatic enrollment contribution would be 3% of employee compensation. The IRS has previously issued rulings that allow employers to automatically enroll employees in employee-sponsored retirement plans. Currently, employees must be notified of the enrollment in advance and permitted to leave the plan at their discretion.

The President's budget also proposes offering employers that participate in automatic enrollment a temporary business tax credit for two years equal to $25 per participating employee up to $250 per year.

The President's budget also proposes doubling a temporary business tax credit available to small employers (those with no more than 100 employees) who sponsor a qualified retirement plan or SIMPLE plan. Currently, small employers can claim a tax credit equal to 50% of the startup cost of sponsoring a plan. The maximum credit is $500 a year for three years. The President's proposal would increase the maximum credit from $500 to $1,000 per year for three years beginning in 2013.

Extend the American Opportunity Tax Credit

The President's budget proposes permanently extending the American Opportunity Tax Credit (AOTC)—a tax benefit for post secondary education—and indexing the eligible expense and income limits for inflation beginning in 2013.[5] The AOTC, which temporarily replaces the Hope credit, was first made available by ARRA for 2009 and 2010. It was extended through 2012 by the Tax Relief, Unemployment Insurance Reauthorization, and Job Creation Act of 2010 (P.L. 111-312). The AOTC allows taxpayers to claim a maximum $2,500 credit for tuition and related expenses (including books). Unlike the Hope credit, which is only available for the first two years of college, the AOTC is available for the first four years of college. In addition, 40% of the AOTC is refundable. The credit is gradually reduced for taxpayers with modified adjusted gross income between $80,000 and $90,000 (between $160,000 and $180,000 if married). Households with modified adjusted gross income above $90,000 ($180,000 if married) are ineligible for the credit.

Exclude Forgiven Student Loan Debt from Income

The President's budget proposes excluding from income certain student loan debt that is currently subject to income tax beginning in 2012. Currently, taxpayers who participate in one of two income-related repayment options offered by the Federal Family Loan and Federal Direct Loan programs must pay tax on any loan amount that is forgiven at the end repayment period. Under the two options available, taxpayers make payments for either 25 years or 10 years (the shorter repayment period is for those working in a qualified public service position).

Any loan balance remaining at the end of repayment period is forgiven, but considered taxable income. The President's proposal would apply to loan balances that remain at the end of the two income repayment related options.

Tax Capital Gains and Dividends of Certain Taxpayers at 20%

The President's budget proposes a 20% tax rate on capital gains and dividends for single taxpayers earning over $200,000 and for married taxpayers earning over $250,000.[6] Prior to 2003, capital gains were taxed at a rate of 20% or 10% depending on one's income. A maximum 18% rate was applied to gains realized on assets held over five years. In addition, dividends were taxed as ordinary income, and therefore subject to the marginal income tax schedule (maximum rate of 39.6%).

In 2003, JGTRRA, initially lowered the rates of taxation on these forms of income to 15% or 10% (again, depending on one's income), and eventually lowered the 10% rate to 0% beginning in 2008. The Tax Increase Prevention and Reconciliation Act of 2005 (TIPRA; P.L. 109-222) extended these rate reductions through the end of 2010. The rates were extended again through 2012 by the Tax Relief, Unemployment Insurance Reauthorization, and Job Creation Act of 2010 (P.L. 111-312). The President's baseline assumes that the 15% and 0% rates will be permanently extended for middle-class taxpayers. The President's proposal would also repeal the maximum 18% rate on longer-held assets.

TAX CUTS FOR BUSINESSES

The tax cuts for businesses that are proposed in the President's budget focus primarily on enhancing the research and experimentation tax credit and expanding the tax incentives for energy investment and manufacturing. Overall, the Administration estimates that the proposed tax incentives for businesses reduce revenues by $46.6 billion over 5 years and $116.4 billion over 10 years.

Eliminate Taxation of Capital Gains on Investments in Qualified Small Business Stock

Under Internal Revenue Code (IRC) Section 1202, non-corporate investors who acquire small business stock at first issue after September 27, 2010, and before January 1, 2012, and hold it for a minimum of five years, may exclude 100% of any gain they realize from the sale or exchange of the stock.

The excluded gain for stock acquired during this period is not considered a preference item under the alternative minimum tax (AMT). For qualified stock acquired between February 18, 2009, and September 27, 2010, the exclusion drops to 75%; but the excluded gains are subject to the AMT. The exclusion reverts to its original level for stock acquired in 2012 and later: 50%.

To qualify for the exclusion, the stock must be issued by a C corporation with gross assets of $50 million or less that is involved in a trade or business outside banking and finance, farming, food and lodging, oil and gas extraction, professional sports, the performing arts, business services (including accounting), health care, law, and architecture.

The President's budget proposes to permanently extend the 100% exclusion for gains on the sale of small business stock and to permanently eliminate the excluded gain as an AMT preference item, as of January 1, 2012. No other changes in the rules governing the use of the exclusion would be made, with one exception.

Taxpayers claiming the exclusion would be required to submit additional information to the Internal Revenue Service (IRS) to ensure they are complying with those rules.

Enhance and Permanently Extend the Research and Experimentation Tax Credit

Under IRC Section 41, companies engaging in or financing qualified research may claim a nonrefundable credit. The credit has four components: (1) a regular credit equal to 20% of qualified research expenditures (QREs) above a base amount linked to a company's ratio of QREs to gross receipts in three of the years from 1984 to 1988, or to 3% of current-year QREs in the case of start-up companies; (2) an alternative simplified credit (ASC) equal to 14% of QREs that exceed 50% of a company's average annual QREs in the three previous tax years, and for companies with no QREs in any of those years, the credit is equal to 6% of current-year QREs; (3) a 20% credit for payments above a base amount to universities to conduct basic research; and (4) a flat 20% credit for payments to consortia engaged in energy research. In the case of the regular credit, the base amount cannot be less than 50% of current-year QREs. The research and experimentation credit, which has been extended 14 times, is due to expire on December 31, 2011. It has an incremental design for the purpose of giving companies an added incentive to undertake more QRE than they otherwise would.

The President's budget proposes to permanently extend the credit and increase the rate for the ASC from 14% to 17%, starting January 1, 2012. These changes may address what critics say are two critical problems with the regular credit: its lack of permanence and a weak incentive effect.[7]

Tax Credit for Investment in Advanced Energy Property

The advanced energy manufacturing tax credit (IRC § 48C) was established under ARRA to encourage investment in domestic clean-energy manufacturing. Under ARRA, $2.3 billion was allocated for tax credits, which were competitively awarded. Projects receiving an award could claim a 30% tax credit for qualified investments in advanced energy manufacturing. Projects were selected based on a broad range of criteria, including commercial viability, potential for domestic job creation, and potential for technological innovation. More than 500 applications, totaling $8 billion in tax credit requests, were received. Ultimately, 183 projects were selected to receive the $2.3 billion that was allocated for this project. The President's budget proposes authorizing an additional $5 billion for Section 48C tax credits.

Tax Credit for Energy Efficient Commercial Building Expenditures

Under current law, taxpayers are allowed a deduction for certain energy-efficiency improvements to commercial building property. A deduction of up to $1.80 per square foot is allowed for qualifying improvements to (1) the interior lighting system; (2) the heating, cooling, ventilation, and hot water system; and (3) the building envelope. A partial deduction is available for improvements made to a single system. The President's budget proposes to enhance the current tax incentives for commercial building energy efficiency by replacing the existing tax deduction with a tax credit. The tax credit would be available for property placed in service during calendar year 2012.

INCENTIVES TO PROMOTE REGIONAL GROWTH

The tax incentives to promote regional growth that are proposed in the President's budget would expand existing regional development programs. Overall, the Administration's proposals to promote regional growth would reduce revenues by $4.7 billion over 5 years and $5.3 billion over 10 years.

Extend and Modify the New Markets Tax Credit (NMTC)

The NMTC is intended to stimulate a greater flow of equity capital into low-income and economically distressed areas by giving investors a tax incentive to invest in community development entities (CDEs). These entities, in turn, are required to invest at least 85% of their tax-preferred capital in projects intended to promote the development of qualified low-income communities. CDEs are certified by a branch of the Treasury Department (the Community Development Financial Institutions Fund or CDFI), and they compete for the right to receive tax-preferred investments.

The NMTC is a nonrefundable tax credit equal to 39% of qualified equity investments (QEIs) in corporations or partnerships that qualify as CDEs. A QEI is an acquisition of stock (in the case of a corporation) or a capital interest (in the case of a partnership) in a CDE that is held for seven years. There is a limit on the share of the credit that a taxpayer can take in each year of that period: 5% of the amount invested in the CDE in the year the investment is made and the following two years, and 6% in each of the next four years, which sum to 39% after seven years. There is also an annual limit on the total amount of tax-preferred investment eligible for the credit. Through the end of 2010, the CDFI has authorized $31 billion in tax-preferred financing; another $5 billion is available for 2011. The NMTC can be used to offset tax liability under the regular income tax but not under the alternative minimum tax (AMT). It is due to expire on December 31, 2011.[8]

The President's budget proposes to extend the NMTC for one year (through the end of 2012) with another allocation of $5 billion. In addition, the proposal would allow any credit taken for QEIs made in 2011 and 2012 to offset AMT liability. These changes would become effective on the date of enactment.

Reform and Expand the Build America Bonds

The President's budget proposal would make the Build America Bonds (BAB) program permanent and lower the credit rate to 28% from the previous 35% rate.[9] The FY2012 budget proposal would also relax the requirement that direct payment BABs (where the issuer receives the tax credit, not the investor) be used only for capital projects. The authority to issue BABs had expired December 31, 2010. Before expiration, $181.2 billion of BABs were issued or roughly one-fifth of total issuance.[10]

Reform and Expand the Low-Income Housing Tax Credit Program

The President's budget proposes amending the rent restriction requirements of the low-income housing tax credit (LIHTC) program. Currently, to qualify for the LIHTC program a property owner must choose between one of two rent restriction requirements: (1) at least 20% of the units must be rent restricted and occupied by tenants with income at or below 50% of area median income (AMI); or at least 40% of the units must be rent restricted and occupied by tenants with incomes at or below 60% of AMI.[11]

The President's budget proposes adding a third choice, which would require that at least 40% of LIHTC units be occupied by tenants with incomes that *average* no more than 60% of AMI. The pool of tenants used to compute this average could not include any tenant with an income over 80% of AMI. In addition, for purposes of computing the average, any tenant whose income is less than 20% of AMI would be treated as if their income were 20% of AMI.

Also included in the President's budget is a proposal to provide a 30% increase in the basis of LIHTC projects financed with tax-exempt bonds, which also preserve the existing affordable housing stock. Enhancing the basis of qualifying projects would increase the amount of LIHTC eligible projects could receive.

Designate Growth Zones

A variety of tax incentives are available under current law to foster the development of certain geographic areas, such as empowerment zones (EZs), enterprise zones, and the Gulf Opportunity Zone (GO Zone). Presently, there are 40 EZs—30 in urban areas and 10 in rural areas—which have been designated as such through a competitive process that has spanned three separate rounds in 1994, 1998, and 2002. Businesses located in an EZ may qualify for several tax benefits, including a 20% wage credit, an enhanced expensing allowance for qualified property placed in service within an EZ, and tax-exempt financing for certain qualified zone facilities.

To be eligible for these benefits, a firm must generate at least 50% of its gross receipts from the active conduct of a qualified line of business within the zone, a substantial portion of its fixed assets must be located within the zone, and at least 35% of its employees must reside there.

The GO Zone encompasses the area devastated by Hurricane Katrina in 2005 that President Bush declared a federal disaster area. Numerous tax incentives were established to facilitate the redevelopment of the zone, but most of them have expired.

Four of the incentives are available through the end of 2011: (1) an increase in available tax-exempt bond financing, (2) an increase in the allocation of low-income housing tax credits, (3) an increase in the rehabilitation credit rate for structures located in the zone, and (4) full expensing for qualified property placed in service in the zone in 2011.

The President's budget proposes replacing this mix of tax incentives for regional economic development with a plan to designate 20 growth zones (14 in urban areas and 6 in rural areas), beginning on January 1, 2012. These designations, which would be chosen through a competitive process by the Secretary of Commerce in consultation with the Secretaries of Agriculture and Housing and Urban Development, would remain in effect from January 1,

2012, through December 31, 2016. A key consideration in the selection process would be an applicant's "competitiveness plan" and its need to attract investment and jobs.

For a plan to succeed, it should clearly explain how its economic strategy would link the zone to regional drivers of economic growth. Two tax incentives would be available for businesses located in a growth zone: (1) a credit equal to 20% of the first $15,000 in wages paid to employees who reside in the zone; the credit drops to 10% for zone residents who are employed outside the zone, and (2) full expensing for qualified property placed in service in the zone.

CONTINUE CERTAIN EXPIRING PROVISIONS THROUGH CALENDAR YEAR 2012

The federal tax code contains numerous temporary provisions, many of which are routinely extended, but not always before they expire. A variety of temporary individual and business tax provisions have already expired or are due to expire on or before December 31, 2011.

These include tax credits for the construction of energy-efficient new homes and the purchase of energy-efficient appliances; an optional deduction for state and local sales taxes; a deduction for qualified tuition and related expenses; an employment credit for native Americans; 15-year straight-line depreciation for qualified leasehold, restaurant, and retail store improvements; and the work opportunity tax credit.

The President's budget proposes to extend over 50 expired or soon-to-expire tax provisions through the end of 2012, at a five-year revenue cost of $20.5 billion. Four provisions account for 55% of the projected cost: incentives for alcohol fuels ($4.8 billion over five years), extension and modification of the IRC Section 25C credit for energy efficiency improvements to existing homes ($1.1 billion), optional deduction for state and local sales taxes ($2.3 billion), and the exception under sub-part F for income derived from active financing ($3.1 billion).

For provisions due to expire at the end of 2011, the extensions would go into effect on January 1, 2012; for those that have already expired or will expire before the end of 2011, the extensions would be retroactive to the date of expiration.

Alternative Minimum Tax (AMT) Relief

The President's budget proposal would patch the Alternative Minimum Tax (AMT) for three years, for 2011 through 2013. The FY2012 budget would pay for this patch by reducing the value of certain tax expenditures through limiting itemized deductions. The budget also includes an alternative "PAYGO" baseline that goes farther than the explicit budget proposal.[12] The PAYGO baseline differs from current law by assuming that certain expiring tax provisions are extended. Under current law, the AMT will revert to the tax year 2000 parameters for the 2011 tax year. The PAYGO baseline in the FY2012 budget assumes the AMT is patched in 2011 and then permanently adjusted for inflation based on 2011 parameters. The result of this alternative PAYGO baseline is an underestimation of the cost in foregone tax collection.

The provision intended to pay for the three-year AMT patch is the limitation on itemized deductions for taxpayers in the highest income tax brackets. Many taxpayers in the 33% tax bracket and all the taxpayers in the 35% bracket would only be allowed to reduce taxable income by an amount equivalent to a taxpayer in the 28% tax bracket. For example, under existing law, a taxpayer in the 33% bracket with $20,000 of itemized deductions would reduce their tax liability by $6,600 ($20,000 multiplied by 33%). Under the FY2012 budget proposal, the same taxpayer would reduce their tax liability by $5,600 ($20,000 multiplied by 28%).

Other Revenue Changes and "Loophole Closers "

The President's budget proposes a range of other proposals that are aimed at reforming the taxation of financial institutions, insurance companies, and U.S. multinational businesses; eliminating tax preferences for fossil fuels; reducing the tax gap; and modifying the estate and gift tax. The Administration estimates that these proposals would increase revenues by $166.2 billion over 5 years and $356.5 billion over 10 years.

Reform Treatment of Financial Institutions and Products

The President's budget proposes four changes to the tax treatment of financial institutions and products. A proposed "financial crisis responsibility" fee would have the largest revenue effect. The fee would be imposed on U.S.-based financial institutions with assets greater than $50 billion and U.S. subsidiaries of international financial institutions with assets greater than $50 billion. The fee would be equal to 7.5 basis points (0.075%) of covered liabilities and would take effect in 2013.

The Administration's other three reform proposals have smaller revenue effects and are somewhat more complicated. One proposal would require corporations that agree to sell their stock at some point in the future in exchange for future compensation to recognize taxable interest income from transactions beginning in 2012. The objective is to create tax parity with corporations that must recognize taxable interest income when they agree to sell their stock now in exchange for future compensation.

Another proposal would require dealers in securities, equity options, commodities, and commodities derivatives to treat the income (or loss) from their dealer activities as ordinary income instead of as 60% long-term capital gain (or loss) and 40% short-term capital gain (or loss) as they currently do. The objective of this proposal is to create tax parity with dealers in other property whose income is treated as ordinary for tax purposes. The Administration's last proposal would modify the definition of "control" to include indirect control relationships for purposes of IRC Section 249, which may disallow or limit the deduction for premiums paid to repurchase debt instruments.

Reinstate Superfund Taxes

Congress appropriates monies from the Superfund Trust Fund to finance the cleanup of contamination from hazardous substances, under the Superfund program administered by the Environmental Protection Agency (EPA).[13] Historically, dedicated industry taxes provided most of the revenues until the taxing authority expired at the end of 1995. These taxes consisted of three excise taxes (one for petroleum, one for certain chemical feedstocks, and one for imported substances made from those same chemicals) and a special environmental tax on corporate income. As the remaining revenues were expended over time, Congress increased the portion of general revenues to help compensate for the loss of the dedicated taxes. General revenues now constitute most, but not all, of the source of revenues for the trust fund. Cost recoveries collected from liable parties, fines and penalties assessed for violations of cleanup requirements, and interest on the unexpended balance of the trust fund continue to contribute monies that augment general revenues. Through EPA enforcement actions, sites with financially viable parties who are liable for the contamination also pay for the cleanup directly using their own funds. These private funds provide additional cleanup resources and help to reserve Superfund appropriations for sites at which the liable parties cannot afford to pay or cannot be found.

Whether to reinstate the dedicated industry taxes has been a long-standing issue since the expiration of the taxing authority at the end of 1995. The debate has involved numerous issues regarding whether the taxes ensure that polluters pay for the cleanup of contamination, or whether the taxes may place an unfair burden of the costs on certain parties who did not cause or contribute to contamination. The Administration proposes reinstating the three excise taxes and the environmental tax on corporate income at the rates that were in effect when the taxes expired at the end of 1995. As a result, an excise tax would be imposed on domestic crude oil and imported petroleum products at a rate of 9.7 cents a barrel; a second excise tax would be imposed on the production of chemical feedstocks at a rate that varies by individual chemical from 22 cents to $4.87 per ton; and an excise tax would be imposed on imported substances made from the same hazardous chemicals targeted by the second excise at the same rate that would have applied if those chemicals had been subject to the feedstocks tax. In addition, corporations would be subject to an environmental income tax equal to 0.12% of the amount by which a corporation's modified alternative minimum taxable income exceeds $2 million. Under the proposal, these taxes would be reinstated on January 1, 2012, and expire on December 31, 2021.

Increase the Oil Spill Liability Trust Fund Financing Rate by One Cent

Under current law, the revenue raised by an excise tax (imposed at a rate of eight cents a barrel through the end of 2016 and nine cents thereafter) on domestic crude oil production and imports of petroleum products is deposited in the Oil Spill Trust Fund (OSTF). Money in the fund is used to pay for the costs associated with the cleanup of oil spills and the economic damage they cause. The funds are also used to help pay for federal oil pollution and prevention and response programs. There is some concern that the balance in the fund may be insufficient to address the costs associated with oil spills similar in magnitude to the Deepwater Horizon spill in 2010.

The Administration proposes raising the rate of the OSTF tax to nine cents a barrel starting January 1, 2012, and then to 10 cents a barrel starting January 1, 2017.

Make the Unemployment Insurance Tax Permanent

Under the Federal Unemployment Tax Act (FUTA), employers are assessed a 6.2% payroll tax on the first $7,000 in wages paid to each employee. This rate includes a 0.2% temporary surtax that Congress first established in 1976 and has extended several times; the current surtax is due to expire on June 30, 2011. Revenue from the tax funds a portion of the unemployment benefits system that is jointly managed by the federal and state governments.

States also impose an unemployment tax on employers. But employers in states that satisfy certain federal requirements may claim a credit for state unemployment taxes equal to as much as 5.4% of the first $7,000 in wages paid to an employee. As a result, the minimum net federal FUTA rate is 0.8%, which consists of a 0.6% permanent tax rate and the temporary surtax rate of 0.2%. The President's budget proposes to permanently extend the 0.2% surtax, as of the date of enactment.

Repeal Last-In, First-Out (LIFO) Method of Accounting for Inventories

Many companies hold inventories of inputs and products for sale. They cannot deduct the cost of inventory items when purchased, because the transactions involve an exchange of cash for assets of equal value. So to compute profits, companies deduct the cost of inventory against the sale of goods. Since identical goods moving out of inventory can have different acquisition costs, companies rely on certain accounting conventions to account for the cost of goods sold.

Most companies use the first-in, first-out method (FIFO) of accounting for the cost of inventory, which assumes that the goods bought first are also the ones sold first. Companies have the option of using the last-in, first-out method (LIFO), which assumes that the goods first purchased make up a company's inventory at the close of the business year. During a period of rising prices, LIFO assigns higher costs to goods sold, reducing current income and the value of year-end inventory. As a result, LIFO can create a tax benefit by allowing taxpayers that hold inventories whose costs are increasing over time to defer taxation of a portion of their income. Use of the LIFO method is not permitted under International Financial Reporting Standards.

The Administration proposes to disallow the use of the LIFO method for federal income tax purposes. Under the proposal, taxpayers that currently use this method would be required to convert their beginning LIFO inventory to its FIFO value in the first tax year starting after December 31, 2012. The resulting rise in gross income would be taken into account ratably over the following 10 years.

Repeal the Gain Limitation for Dividends Received in Reorganization Exchanges

When a shareholder receives both stock and non-stock considerations in a reorganization under IRC Section 368, IRC Section 356 applies to any gains from the transaction.

Under IRC Section 356, any gain realized by a taxpayer on an exchange of stock in a target company for stock in an acquiring company and cash (or boot) is recognized to the extent of the cash received (the so-called boot-within-a-gain limitation). In addition, the recognized gain is taxed as a dividend if the exchange is equivalent to the distribution of a dividend and the acquiring company has sufficient earnings and profits; the remainder of the recognized gain is considered a long-term capital gain. No loss is recognized on the exchange.

These rules mean that the shareholder exchanging the stock has a taxable income from the transaction that is equal to the lesser of the cash received or the total gain realized on the exchange, and this income is either capital gain or dividend income, depending on the facts and circumstances.

The Administration is asking Congress to repeal the boot-within-a-gain limitation when an exchange of stock under a Section 368 reorganization is equivalent to the distribution of a dividend. In seeking the change, the Administration wants to make the tax treatment of dividends more uniform and prevent the repatriation of the profits held by foreign subsidiaries of U.S. corporations with minimal taxation through reorganizations. The proposal would go into effect on January 1, 2012.

Reform U.S. International Tax System

The tax proposals made in the FY2012 budget request reflect the Administration's priorities for international tax reform. Several proposals for repeal of certain incentives would raise substantial revenue. Proponents argue that these measures will help close the tax gap. Opponents have expressed concerns over their effect on economic growth and competitiveness.[14] Taken together, the Administration estimates that they will raise an additional $65.0 billion over 5 years and $129.2 over 10 years.

Defer Deduction of Expenses Related to Deferred Income

U.S. parent firms can deduct expenses of foreign subsidiaries, such as interest, while not recognizing income from those foreign subsidiaries that is not repatriated (not paid to the parent as dividends).[15] U.S. parents can thus benefit from deductions, while not including earnings in income. The President's budget proposal would defer the deduction of a portion of these costs until the income is repatriated. This proposal would be effective beginning in 2012.

Reform Foreign Tax Credit

U.S. firms with operations abroad are allowed a tax credit against their U.S. income tax liability for foreign taxes paid on foreign income currently subject to tax.[16] Foreign tax credits may be claimed on an "overall" basis, so that income and tax credits from all countries are combined. As a result, "cross-crediting," where credits paid in excess of U.S. tax in one country may be used to offset U.S. tax in a country where the foreign tax is lower than the U.S. tax, may occur. By applying excess credits generated in a high tax country to earnings repatriated from a low tax country, firms can avoid most U.S. tax.

Under the President's proposal, a U.S. firm would be required to determine its deemed paid foreign tax credit on a consolidated basis based on the aggregate foreign taxes and earnings and profits of all of the foreign subsidiaries with respect to which the U.S. taxpayer can claim a deemed paid foreign tax. This proposal would be effective beginning in 2012.

Tax Currently Excess Returns Associated with Transfers of Intangibles Offshore

Transactions between related parties, in particular transfers to low-taxed affiliates, can generate significant tax savings for U.S.-based multinational firms. The Administration's FY2012 budget proposal would provide that any excess income generated by such a transfer be included in subpart F income (subpart F income refers to income earned by foreign affiliates of majority owned U.S. firms). Excess income is defined as the excess of gross income beyond what the properly apportioned and allocated costs to generate this income would merit. The proposal would be effective for transactions beginning January 1, 2012.

Limit Shifting of Income Through Intangible Property Transfers

The President's budget proposes clarifying the definition of intangible property and the allocation of income and deductions among the parties involved. Taxpayers may sell, lease, or otherwise transfer intangible property to foreign corporations. If the appropriate royalty or other arms-length payment for use of the property is not made, profits can be artificially shifted to low tax jurisdictions. The President's proposes clarifying some regulations to try to reduce this scope of this shifting. The proposal would be effective for transactions beginning January 1, 2012.

Disallow the Deduction for Excess Non-Taxed Reinsurance Premiums Paid to Affiliates

U.S. insurance companies pay for reinsurance through premiums paid to a reinsurer. The premium payments are deductible expenses for the U.S insurance company. If the payment is in the form of income producing asset, the income generated by the asset is taxable if the reinsurer is a U.S. company. If, however, the reinsurer is a foreign company, this income would avoid U.S. income taxes. For reinsurance premiums paid to a foreign reinsurer, the U.S. levies an excise tax of 1% on the premium paid.

The 1% excise tax is still significantly less than the income tax that would be paid if the reinsurer were a U.S. company. The Administration's FY2012 budget proposal would deny the deduction for reinsurance premium payments if paid to a foreign reinsurer. The provision would also exclude from the U.S. insurance company's income any reinsurance recovered from reinsurance paid for with non-deductible premiums. The proposal would be effective beginning January 1, 2012.

Limit Earnings Stripping by Expatriated Entities

A number of high profile U.S. based companies have recently realized tax savings by nominally becoming foreign based companies through a process known as inversion or expatriation.[17] After completing the inversion, the companies new "parent" is technically located outside the United States, while the old "parent" is a subsidiary operating within the United States. The new foreign based parent may then loan money to its U.S. subsidiary. The U.S. subsidiary is able to lower its U.S. tax liability by deducting the interest payments on the loan. The President's budget proposes to limit this practice, known as earnings stripping, by disallowing the deduction for interest on loans made within an inverted entity in instances where interest deductions are large relative to income. The proposal would be effective beginning January 1, 2012.

Modify Tax Rules for Dual Capacity Taxpayers

U.S. taxpayers are allowed a tax credit against their U.S. income tax liability for foreign taxes paid. The credit, known as the foreign tax credit, is intended to alleviate the double taxation of income. In some instances, foreign taxes that are paid are in exchange for a direct economic benefit provided by the foreign government. An example are payments that are effectively royalty for the extraction of oil and gas. Taxpayers involved in a such an exchange are referred to as dual capacity taxpayers, and are generally disallowed the foreign tax credit by U.S. regulations. The President's budget proposes to tighten the foreign tax credit rules that apply to dual capacity earners.

Reform Treatment of Insurance Companies and Products

The President budget proposes to modify the taxation of insurance companies and selected insurance products through three specific proposals. Taken together, the Administration estimates that they will raise an additional $3.7 billion over 5 years and $14.1 over 10 years.

Modify Rules that Apply to the Sales of Life Insurance Contracts

Under current law, an exclusion from Federal income tax is provided for amounts received from a life insurance contract paid by reason of the death of the insured. If the rights to the proceeds of the contract are sold prior to the insured's death (a life settlement transaction), this exclusion is limited and the transaction may be taxable. The President's budget proposes to expand information reporting for these transactions. The proposal is likely directed at reducing the portion of the tax gap associated with non reporting or under reporting of this income. The proposal would take effect for tax years beginning in 2012.

Modify Dividends-Received Deduction for Life Insurance Company Separate Accounts

The President's budget proposes to simplify the regime which restricts the ability of insurance companies to fund tax deductible reserve increases with tax preferred income. This provision may be attempting to reduce the tax differences between life insurance companies and other companies, which, generally, can not engage in this type of tax arbitrage. The proposal would take effect for tax years beginning in 2012.

Expand Pro-Rate Interest Expense Disallowance for Corporate-Owned Life Insurance (COLI)

The President's budget proposes to eliminate the exception under the pro rata interest deduction disallowance rule for employees, officers and directors—for all but 20-percent owners. As with the prior provision, this provision may be attempting to restrict a tax arbitrage opportunity. The proposal would take effect for tax years beginning in 2012.

Eliminate Fossil-Fuel Tax Preferences

President Obama agreed at the G-20 Summit in Pittsburgh in September 2009 to phase out fossil-fuel subsidies. The Leaders' Statement from the Pittsburgh Summit noted "Inefficient fossil fuel subsidies encourage wasteful consumption, reduce our energy security, impede investment in clean energy sources and undermine efforts to deal with the threat of climate change."[18] The President's FY2012 budget proposes to eliminate tax preferences for coal and oil and gas. The Administration estimates elimination of the fossil-fuel tax preferences will raise an additional $24.0 billion over 5 years and $46.2 over 10 years.

Eliminate Coal Preferences

Expensing of Exploration and Development Costs

Special rules allow taxpayers to expense costs associated with identifying and locating ore or mineral deposits, including coal. Generally, costs that benefit future periods must be capitalized and recovered over time. Allowing coal-related exploration and development costs to be expensed encourages investment in coal production. The FY2012 budget proposes to change the tax treatment of coal-related exploration and development costs, so that such costs are capitalized and deducted over time according to generally applicable rules. Such a change would make cost recovery for coal investments similar to cost recovery in other industries. This proposal would be effective beginning December 31, 2011.

Percentage Depletion for Hard Mineral Fossil Fuels

Firms that extract coal and other hard-mineral fossil fuels are permitted a deduction to recover their capital investment in a mineral reserve, which depreciates due to the physical and economic depletion or exhaustion as the mineral is recovered. Depletion, like depreciation, is a form of capital recovery. One method for computing the deduction is the percentage depletion.[19] Under percentage depletion, the deduction for recovery of capital investment is a fixed percentage of the "gross income"—namely, revenue—from the sale of the mineral. Typically, despite limitations, total deductions under this method exceed the capital invested to acquire and develop the reserve. By reducing tax rates, percentage depletion encourages investment in coal and other hard-mineral fossil fuels. The FY2012 budget proposes to eliminate percentage depletion, allowing fossil-fuel producers to instead claim cost depletion. This proposal would be effective beginning December 31, 2011.

Capital Gains Treatment for Royalties

Royalties from certain dispositions of coal are treated as long-term capital gains, and thereby taxed at a reduced rate. Generally, royalties are taxed at ordinary rates. The favorable capital gains treatment of coal royalties encourages investment in coal. The FY2012 budget proposes eliminating the capital gains treatment of coal royalties. This proposal would be effective beginning December 31, 2011.

Domestic Manufacturing Deduction for Coal and other Hard-Mineral Fossil Fuels

A deduction is allowed with respect to income attributable to domestic production activities (IRC Section 199). The deduction is generally equal to 9% of the lesser of qualified production activities income or taxable income. Under current law, qualified income includes income generated from the sale, exchange, or disposition of coal or other hard-mineral fossil fuels. The Section 199 deduction reduces the effective tax rate for qualified activities, encouraging investment in such activities. The FY2012 budget proposes to exclude from the definition of qualified activities the sale, exchange, or disposition of coal and other hard-mineral fossil fuels. This proposal would be effective beginning December 31, 2011.

Eliminate Oil and Gas Preferences

Enhanced Oil Recovery Credit

A 15% credit is available for qualifying enhanced oil recovery (EOR) costs. Qualifying EOR costs include the costs of tangible equipment; intangible drilling and development costs; and deductible tertiary injectant costs. The credit is phased out once the price of oil exceeds the legislatively determined reference price. In recent years, the price of oil has been high enough such that the EOR credit has been fully phased out. The FY2012 budget proposes to repeal the EOR credit. This proposal would be effective beginning December 31, 2011.

Credit for Oil and Gas Produced from Marginal Wells

Production of crude oil and natural gas from marginal wells are eligible for a tax credit. A marginal well is defined under IRC Section 45I(c)(3). The maximum credit amount is $3 per barrel of qualified oil production and $0.50 per 1,000 cubic feet of qualified gas production. The credit is phased out once the price of oil exceeds the legislatively determined reference price. In recent years, the price of oil has been high enough such that the EOR credit has been fully phased out. The FY2012 budget proposes to repeal the credit for production from marginal wells. This proposal would be effective beginning December 31, 2011.

Expensing of Intangible Drilling Costs

Intangible drilling costs (IDCs) are expenditures paid by the firms engaged in the exploration and development of oil, gas, or geothermal properties for fuel, labor, repairs to drilling equipment, materials, hauling, and supplies. Under current law, IDCs may be partially or fully expensed (deducted in the year they are incurred) rather than capitalized (recovered over time through depletion or depreciation). The option to expense IDCs applies to domestic properties, which include certain off-shore wells (essentially those within the exclusive economic zone of the United States), generally including offshore platforms. The FY2012 budget proposes eliminating the expensing allowance for IDCs. Instead, IDCs would be capitalized and the costs recovered over time. This proposal would be effective beginning December 31, 2011.

Deduction for Tertiary Injectants

Current law allows taxpayers to claim a deduction for the cost of qualifying tertiary injectants. Tertiary injectants are used as part of a tertiary recovery method to increase the recovery of crude oil. The FY2012 budget proposes to eliminate the deduction for tertiary injectants. This proposal would be effective beginning December 31, 2011.

Exception to Passive Loss Limitations for Working Interests in Oil and Natural Gas Properties

Losses by a taxpayer with a passive ownership interest in a business are generally not deductible against other forms of income. Unused passive losses may be carried forward to offset passive income in the future. In general, a passive interest is one in which the taxpayer does not materially participate in the business's operation. One exception is the ownership of a working interest in an oil or natural gas property. The owner of a working interest may deduct losses from such interest against other (non-passive) income. The FY2012 budget proposes to eliminate the exception to passive loss limitations for working interests in oil and natural gas property. This proposal would be effective beginning December 31, 2011.

Percentage Depletion for Oil and Natural Gas

Firms that extract oil, gas, or other minerals are permitted a deduction to recover their capital investment in a mineral reserve, which depreciates due to the physical and economic depletion or exhaustion as the mineral is recovered. Depletion, like depreciation, is a form of capital recovery.

One method for computing the deduction is the percentage depletion.[20] Under percentage depletion, the deduction for recovery of capital investment is a fixed percentage of the "gross income"—namely, revenue—from the sale of the mineral. Typically, despite limitations, total deductions under this method exceed the capital invested to acquire and develop the reserve. The FY2012 budget proposes to eliminate percentage depletion, allowing oil and gas producers to instead claim cost depletion. This proposal would be effective beginning December 31, 2011.

Domestic Manufacturing Deduction for Oil and Natural Gas Companies

A deduction is allowed with respect to income attributable to domestic production activities (IRC § 199). The deduction is generally equal to 9% of the lesser of qualified production activities income or taxable income. The deduction for income from oil and gas properties is limited to 6%. Under current law, qualified income includes income generated from the sale, exchange, or disposition of oil, natural gas, or primary products thereof. The Section 199 deduction reduces the effective tax rate for qualified activities, encouraging investment in such activities. The FY2012 budget proposes to exclude from the definition of qualified activities the sale, exchange, or disposition of oil, natural gas, or primary products thereof. This proposal would be effective beginning December 31, 2011.

Increase Geological and Geophysical Amortization Period for Independent Producers

The amortization period for geological and geophysical expenditures for independent oil and gas producers is two years and seven years for integrated oil and gas producers. Geological and geophysical expenditures are costs associated with obtaining and accumulating data on mineral properties. A reduced amortization period allows these costs to be recovered over a shorter period of time, encouraging investment. The FY2012 budget proposes to increase the amortization period for geological and geophysical expenditures for independent oil and gas producers from two to seven years. This proposal would be effective beginning December 31, 2011.

Tax Carried (Profits) Interest as Ordinary Income

A partnership does not pay income taxes, instead gains and losses flow through to the partners who include it on their income tax returns. The income from the partnership is often taxed as capital gains or qualified dividends at reduced tax rates (i.e., 15%). Some partners receive partnership interests in exchange for contributions of capital (that is, investments) and are limited partners; some partners receive partnership interests in exchange for services (carried interests) and these are general partners who actively manage the partnership. The Administration is proposing to designate a general partner's share of partnership income that is not attributable to invested capital as ordinary income, which would be taxed at the higher individual income tax rates rather than at the reduced capital gains tax rate. In addition, this share of income would be subject to self-employment taxes. The Administration projects this tax change will increase tax revenues by $10.1 billion over 5 years and $14.8 billion over 10 years.

Deny Deduction for Punitive Damages

Under certain circumstances, punitive damages paid a taxpayer can be deducted. The deduction is allowed for damages paid as ordinary and necessary expenses in carrying on a business. The Administration has proposed not allowing a deduction for punitive damages paid, arguing the deduction undermines the role that damages play in discouraging and penalizing undesirable activities. This proposal is projected to increase tax revenues by $127 million over 5 years and $312 million over 10 years.

Repeal Lower-of-Cost-or-Market Inventory Accounting Method

A taxpayer maintaining inventories (e.g., a business holding unsold goods) may use a variety of methods to determine the end of accounting period cost of the inventories. One method is the lower-of-cost-or-market (LCM) method, and it is argued this method understates taxable income. The method basically allows losses on inventory to be recognized and deducted against income for tax purposed without an actual transaction taking place (an unrealized loss), but unrealized gains are not recognized and added to income. The Administration argues that this asymmetric treatment of inventory valuation is unwarranted and proposes to prohibit the use of the LCM method. This proposal is projected to increase tax revenues by $5.5 billion over 5 years and $8.1 billion over 10 years.

Simplify the Tax Code

The Administration has proposed 11 relatively minor items to simplify the tax code. These items mostly reduce the burden of administering some tax provisions (and reducing tax avoidance) or reduce the complexity of certain provisions for taxpayers. The items would affect tax provisions dealing with the plug-in electric-drive motor vehicle credit, individual retirement accounts, employee stock option plans, partnerships, publicly-traded REITs, and private foundations. In addition, three items would reduce the complexity and compliance burdens of tax-exempt bonds on State and local governments. These items are projected to increase tax revenues by $148 million over 5 years and decrease tax revenues by $407 million over 10 years.

Reduce The Tax Gap and Make Reforms

The President's budget contains a number of proposals aimed at reducing the tax gap and making other reforms. The proposals are intended to expand information reporting, improve tax compliance, strengthen tax administration, and modify the estate and gift tax. The proposed changes are estimated to increase tax revenues by $7.8 billion over 5 years and $20.9 billion over 10 years.

Expand Information Reporting

The Internal Revenue Service (IRS) has found that third-party information reporting reduces tax evasion because the IRS can match data on the information reporting forms with data reported by taxpayers. Over the years, the number of information reporting forms has greatly increased. Better information reporting, however, imposes higher compliance costs on taxpayers, reduces the privacy of taxpayers, and raises IRS administrative costs.

Repeal and Modify Information Reporting on Payments to Corporations and Payments for Property

The Patient Protection and Affordable Care Act (P.L. 111-148) expanded the information reporting requirement to include payments by taxpayers to a corporation (except a tax-exempt corporation) and payments for property. The proposal would repeal the information reporting requirement in P.L. 111-148 because the number and complexity of corporate taxpayers have increased, some taxpayers would have compliance issues, and some small businesses would have an undue compliance burden.

The proposal would require businesses to file an information return for payments for services to a corporation (except a tax-exempt corporation). Information returns would not be required for payments for property. This reduced reporting requirement would have a net effect of lowering federal revenue. The proposal would be effective for payments made after December 31, 2011.

Require Information Reporting for Private Separate Accounts of Life Insurance Companies

Policyholders of life insurance are not eligible for tax-free or tax-deferred income if they have control—through a life insurance company—over investments in a separate account to the degree that the policyholder, and not the insurance company, is considered the owner of the investments. In some cases, private separate accounts are being used to avoid income tax that would be due if the assets were held directly.

The proposal would require life insurance companies to report information to the IRS, for each contract whose cash value is partially or wholly invested in a private separate account for any portion of the taxable year and represents at least 10% of the value of the account. The proposal would be effective for taxable years beginning after December 31, 2011.

Require a Certified Taxpayer Identification Number (TIN) from Contractors and Allow Certain Withholding

Currently, the IRS does not have accurate taxpayer identifying information on contractors, because of inadequate information reporting. The proposal would require a contractor receiving payments of $600 or more in a calendar year from a particular business to furnish to the business the contractor's certified TIN. A business would be required to verify the contractor's TIN with the IRS, which would be authorized to disclose, solely for this purpose, whether the certified TIN-name combination matches IRS records.

If a contractor failed to furnish an accurate certified TIN, the business would be required to withhold a flat-rate percentage of gross payments. The proposal would be effective for payments made to contractors after December 31, 2011.

Improve Compliance by Businesses

Require Greater Electronic Filing of Returns

Currently, those corporations, partnerships, and tax-exempt organizations, that have assets of $10 million or more and file annually more than 250 returns, are required to file Schedule M-3 electronically. Generally, compliance increases when taxpayers are required to provide better information to the IRS in usable form.

Large organizations with assets of $10 million or more generally maintain financial records in electronic form. The proposal would require all corporations and partnerships that must file Schedule M-3 to file their income tax returns electronically. The proposal would be effective for taxable years ending after December 31, 2011.

Authorize the Department of the Treasury to Require Additional Information to Be Included in Electronically Filed Form 5500 Annual Reports

Currently sponsors of a funded plan of deferred compensation (or the administrator of the plan) and certain pension and welfare benefit plans (under ERISA) are required to file an annual report (Form 5500 and attachments) disclosing certain information to the Department of Labor (DOL). The proposal would provide the IRS with the authority to require that the electronically filed annual reports include information that is relevant only to employee benefit plan tax requirements. This additional electronic filing of information will assist the IRS in improving tax compliance. The proposal would be effective for plan years beginning after December 31, 2011.

Implement Standards Clarifying When Employee Leasing Companies Can Be Held Liable for Their Clients' Federal Employment Taxes

Employee leasing is the practice of contracting with an outside business to handle certain administrative, personnel, and payroll matters for a taxpayer's employees. Employee leasing companies typically prepare and file employment tax returns for their clients using the leasing company's name and employer identification number, often taking the position that the leasing company is the statutory or common law employer of their clients' workers. The proposal would set forth standards for holding employee leasing companies jointly liable with their clients for federal employment taxes. The proposal would also provide standards for holding employee leasing companies solely liable for such taxes if they meet specified requirements. The provision would be effective for employment tax returns required to be filed with respect to wages paid after December 31, 2011.

Increase Certainty with Respect to Worker Classification

Under current tax law, workers must be classified into one of two mutually exclusive categories: employees or self-employed (sometimes referred to as independent contractors). A business owner must withhold and remit income taxes, Social Security and Medicare taxes; and pay unemployment taxes on wages paid to an employee. In contrast, a business owner does not have to withhold and remit taxes or pay unemployment taxes on payments to independent contractors.

Worker classification generally is based on a common-law test for determining whether an employment relationship exists. Under common-law rules, a worker is an employee if the employer can control what the worker does and how the worker does it. Currently, the IRS states that three categories of common-law rules provide evidence of the degree of control and independence: behavior, financial, and type of relationship. The definition of "employee" has been affected by IRC Section 530 "Safe Harbor Rules," which were enacted in the Revenue Act of 1978 (P.L. 95-600). If an employer qualifies for the safe harbor rules, then generally the employer is allowed to treat a worker as not being an employee for employment tax purposes, regardless of the individual's actual status under the common-law test.

Employers are more likely to withhold and submit taxes than independent contractors are to voluntarily pay their tax liabilities, consequently the misclassification of employees as independent contractors contributes to the tax gap.

The proposal would permit the IRS to require prospective reclassification of workers who are currently misclassified and whose reclassification has been prohibited under current law. The Department of the Treasury and the IRS also would be permitted to issue generally applicable guidance on the proper classification of workers under common law standards. This would enable service recipients to properly classify workers with much less concern about future IRS examinations. Treasury and the IRS would be directed to issue guidance interpreting common law in a neutral manner recognizing that many workers are, in fact, not employees.

The proposal would be effective upon enactment, but prospective reclassification of those covered by current special provision would not be effective until the first calendar year beginning at least one year after date of enactment. The transition period could be up to two years for independent contractors with existing written contracts establishing their status.

Repeal Special Estimated Tax Payment Provision for Certain Insurance Companies

Under current law, an insurance company uses reserve accounting to compute losses incurred. That is, losses incurred for the taxable year includes losses paid during the taxable year (net of salvage and reinsurance recovered), plus or minus the increase or decrease in discounted unpaid losses during the year. An adjustment is also made for the change in discounted estimated salvage and reinsurance recoverable. Unpaid losses are determined on a discounted basis to account for the time that may elapse between an insured loss event and the payment or other resolution of the claim. Taxpayers may, however, elect under IRC Section 847 to take an additional deduction equal to the difference between the amount of their reserves computed on a discounted basis and the amount computed on an undiscounted basis.

Although this provision is revenue neutral, it imposes a substantial recordkeeping burden on both taxpayers and the IRS. The proposal would repeal IRC Section 847, and the entire balance of any existing special loss discount account would be included in gross income.

In lieu of immediate inclusion in gross income for the first taxable year beginning after December 31, 2011, taxpayers would be permitted to elect to include the balance of any existing special loss discount account in gross income ratable over a four taxable year period, beginning with the first taxable year beginning after December 31, 2011.

Repeal Special Rules Modifying the Amount of Estimated Tax Payments by Corporations

Under IRC Section 6655, corporations generally are required to pay their income tax liability for a taxable year in quarterly estimated payments. A number of acts have modified this standard rules as to the amount due by "large corporations" for a particular quarter. The frequent changes to the corporate estimated tax payment schedule do not generally increase a corporation's income tax liability for a particular taxable year. However, the frequency of such changes operates to increase uncertainty within the corporate tax system. The proposal would repeal all legislative acts that cause the amount and timing of corporate estimated payments to differ from the rules described under Section 6655. The proposal would be effective for taxable years beginning after December 31, 2011.

Strengthen Tax Administration

Revise Offer-in-Compromise Application Rules

Current law provides that the IRS may compromise any civil or criminal case arising under the internal revenue laws prior to a reference to the Department of Justice for prosecuting or defense. In 2006, a new provision was enacted to require taxpayers to make certain nonrefundable payments with an initial offer-in-compromise of a tax case. Requiring nonrefundable payments with an offer-in-compromise may substantially reduce access to the offer-in-compromise program. The proposal would eliminate the requirements that an initial offer-in-compromise include a nonrefundable payment of any portion of the taxpayer's offer. The proposal would be effective for offers-in-compromise submitted after the date of enactment.

Expand Internal Revenue Service Access to Information in the National Directory of New Hires for Tax Administration Purposes

Under current law, the Office of Child Support Enforcement of the Department of Health and Human Services maintains the National Directory of New Hires (NDNH), which is a database that contains data from Form W-4 for newly-hired employees, quarterly wage data from state workforce and federal agencies for all employees, and unemployment insurance data from state workforce agencies for all individuals who have applied for or received unemployment benefits. Under current provisions of the Social Security Act, the IRS may obtain data from the NDNH, but only for the purpose of administering the earned income tax credit (EITC) and verifying employment reported on a tax return. Employment data are useful to the IRS in administering a wide range of tax provisions beyond the EITC. The proposal would amend the Social Security Act to expand IRS access to NDNH data for general tax administration purposes. The proposal would be effective upon enactment.

Make Repeated Willful Failure to File a Tax Return a Felony

Current law provides that willful failure to file a tax return is a misdemeanor. A taxpayer who fails to file returns for multiple years commits a separate misdemeanor offense for each year. Increased criminal penalties would help to deter multiple willful failures to file tax returns. The proposal would provide that any person who willfully fails to file tax returns in any three years within any five consecutive year period, if the aggregated tax liability for such period is at least $50,000, would classify such failure as a felony. The proposal would be effective for returns required to be filed after December 31, 2011.

Facilitate Tax Compliance with Local Jurisdictions

Although federal tax returns and return information (FTI) generally are confidential, the IRS and the Treasury Department may share FTI with states as well as certain local government entities that are treated as states for this purpose. Generally, the purpose of information sharing is to facilitate tax administration. Indian Tribal Governments (ITGs) are not treated as states for purposes of information sharing. IRS and Treasury compliance activity, especially with respect to alcohol, tobacco, and fuel excise taxes, may necessitate information sharing with ITGs. For purposes of information sharing, the proposal would treat as states those ITGs that impose alcohol, tobacco, or fuel excise, or income, or wage taxes, to the extent necessary for

ITG tax administration. The proposal would be effective for disclosures made after enactment.

Extend Statute of Limitations Where State Adjustment Affects Federal Tax Liability

In general, additional federal tax liabilities in the form of tax, interest, penalties and additions to tax must be assessed by the IRS within three years after the date a return is filed. The general statute of limitations serves as a barrier to the effective use by the IRS of state and local tax adjustment reports when the reports are provided by the state or local revenue agency to the IRS with little time remaining for assessments to be made at the federal level. The proposal would create an additional exception to the general three-year statute of limitations for assessment of federal tax liability resulting from adjustments to state or local tax liability. The proposal would be effective for returns required to be filed after December 31, 2011.

Improve Investigative Disclosure Statute

Generally, tax return information is confidential, unless a specific exception in the Code applies. In the case of tax administration, the Code permits Treasury and IRS officers and employees to disclose return information to the extent necessary to obtain information not otherwise reasonably available, in the course of an audit or investigation, as prescribed by regulation. Treasury regulations effective since 2003 state that the term "necessary" in this context does not mean essential or indispensable, but rather appropriate and helpful in obtaining the information sought. The proposal would clarify the taxpayer privacy law by stating that the law does not prohibit Treasury and IRS officers and employees from identifying themselves, their organizational affiliation, and the nature and subject of an investigation, when contacting third parties in connection with a civil or criminal tax investigation. The proposal would be effective for disclosures make after enactment.

Require Taxpayers Who Prepare Their returns Electronically but File Their Returns on Paper to Print Their Returns with a 2-D Bar Code

Taxpayers can prepare their tax returns electronically and, instead of filing their returns electronically, may print out a paper copy and file the return on paper by mailing it to the IRS. The proposal would require all taxpayers who prepare their tax returns electronically but print their returns and file them on paper to print their returns with a 2-D bar code that can be scanned by the IRS to convert the paper return into an electronic format. The proposal would be effective for tax returns filed after December 31, 2011.

Require Prisons Located in the United States to Provide Information to the Internal Revenue Service

The IRS is unable to cross reference tax returns received with a list of prison inmates to determine whether inmates are claiming tax benefits to which they are not entitled. The IRS has become aware that some incarcerated individuals are claiming tax benefits to which they may not be entitled. The proposal would require all prisons located in the United States to submit to the IRS, by December 1 of each year, a list of names and validated Social Security numbers of all inmates serving sentences of one year or more. The proposal would be effective upon enactment.

Allow the Internal Revenue Service (IRS) to Absorb Credit and Debit Card Processing Fees for Certain Tax Payments

IRC Section 6311 permits the IRS to receive payment of taxes by any commercially acceptable means that the Secretary deems appropriate. When taxpayers agree to make additional payments during in telephone consultations with IRS agents, it is inefficient for both taxpayers and the IRS to require taxpayers to contact a third party service provider to make credit and debit card payments. The proposal would amend Section 6311(d) to allow the IRS to accept credit or debit card payments directly from taxpayers and to absorb the credit and debit card processing fees for certain tax payments, without charging a separate processing fee to the taxpayer. The proposal would be effective for payments make after the date of enactment.

Expand Penalties

Impose a Penalty on Failure to Comply with Electronic Filing Requirements

Certain corporations and tax-exempt organizations (including certain charitable trusts and private foundations) are required to file their returns electronically. Although there are additions to tax for the failure to file returns, there is no specific penalty for a failure to comply with a requirement to file electronically. The proposal would establish an assessable penalty for a failure to comply with a requirement of electronic format for a return that is filed. The proposal would be effective for returns required to be electronically filed after December 31, 2011.

Increase Penalty Imposed on Paid Preparers who Fail to Comply with Earned Income Tax Credit (EITC) Due Diligence Requirements

IRC Section 6695(g) imposes a $100 penalty on tax return preparers who fail to comply with the due diligence requirements imposed by regulations with respect to determining eligibility for, or the amount of, the EITC for each such failure. The IRS estimates that as many as a quarter of EITC claims are made in error. The proposal would increase the Section 6695(g) penalty from $100 to $500. The proposal would be effective for returns required to be filed after December 31, 2011.

Estate Tax

The President's budget proposal uses a policy baseline that would return the estate and gift tax parameters to those in place for the 2009 tax year for decedents in 2013 and beyond.[21] Specifically, under the alternative policy baseline, in 2013, the exemption amount would be $3.5 million. For 2011 and 2012, under P.L. 111-312, the exemption amount is $5 million with spouses allowed to transfer any unused exemption amount to the surviving spouse, creating the equivalent of a $10 million exemption. The spousal transfer is typically referred to as portability. The budget proposes making the portability provision described above permanent. Thus, under the alternative policy baseline, the $3.5 exemption amount would become the equivalent of a $7 million exemption for married decedents.[22]

In addition to extending the portability option, the FY2012 budget includes additional modifications to estate taxes. First is a provision that would require inheritors to use the same basis (or value) for transferred assets from an estate when calculating future income tax liability. A second provision would make it more difficult to reduce the valuation of a transferred asset. Under current law, the value jointly held assets that include restrictions on resale can be reduced because the estate would not receive full market value with the restrictions. The budget proposal would identify certain restrictions that are under family control and that can be easily removed after death. These "soft" restrictions would be disregarded when determining valuation discounts.

Two more provisions are much more complicated, but are intended to close estate tax loopholes. The first would limit the value of so-called grantor annuity trusts (GRATs) and the second would modify the rules covering generation skipping taxes (GSTs) to make it more difficult to avoid estate taxes through multigenerational trust arrangements. These provisions are in response to popular tax planning techniques intended to reduce estate tax liability.

COST ESTIMATES

The Administration has estimated the cost of the President's FY2012 budget proposals. Table 1 presents the 5- and 10-year estimates.

Table 1. The Administration's Cost Estimates for the President's FY2012 Budget Proposals (all figures are in millions of dollars)

Provision	2012-2016	2012-2021
Tax Cuts For Families And Individuals	-91,928	-253,563
Expand earned income credit	-4,414	-12,313
Expand child and dependent care tax credit	-4,452	-9,605
Automatic enrollment in IRAs, employer enrollment tax credit, and small employer plan tax credit	-4,021	-14,378
Extend the American opportunity tax credit	-33,806	-93,596
Exclude forgiven student loan debt from income	-	-
Tax capital gains and dividends of certain taxpayers at 20%	-45,235	-123,671
Tax Cuts for Businesses	-46,630	-116,381
Eliminate taxation of capital gains on investments in qualified small business stock	-	-5,417
Enhance and permanently extend the research and experimentation tax credit	-41,785	-106,278
Tax credit for investment in advanced energy property	-3,820	-3,661
Tax credit for energy efficient commercial building expenditures	-1,025	-1,025
Incentives to Promote Regional Growth	-4,703	-5,253
Extend and modify the New Markets Tax Credit (NMTC)	-858	-1,870
Reform and expand the Build American Bonds	-13	-28
Reform and expand the Low-Income Housing Tax Credit (LIHTC)	-176	-872
program		
Designate growth zones	-3,656	-2,483
Continue Certain Expiring Provisions Through Calendar Year 2012	-21,682	-22,321
Pay for Alternative Minimum Tax (AMT) Relief	113,884	321,291
Other Revenue Changes and Loophole Closers:	166,153	356,481
Reform treatment of financial institutions and products	11,304	33,216
Reinstate Superfund taxes	9,575	20,819
Increase the oil spill liability trust fund financing rate by one cent	219	451
Make the unemployment tax permanent	7,217	15,015
Repeal LIFO method of accounting for inventories	21,188	52,880

Table 1. (Continued)

Provision	2012-2016	2012-2021
Repeal the gain limitation for dividends received in reorganization exchanges	377	849
Reform U.S. international tax system:		
-Defer deduction of expenses related to deferred income	25,017	37,665
-Reform foreign tax credit	22,243	51,444
-Tax currently excess returns associated with transfers of intangibles offshore	9,848	20,831
-Limit shifting of income through intangible property transfers	448	1,668
- Disallow the deduction for excess non-taxed reinsurance premiums paid to affiliates	1,103	2,614
-Limit earnings stripping by expatriated entities	1,780	4,222
Reform treatment of Insurance Companies and Products:		
-Modify rules that apply to the sales of life insurance contracts	344	1,243
-Modify dividends-received deduction for life insurance company separate accounts	2,368	5,146
-Expand pro-rate interest expense disallowance for corporate-owned life insurance (COLI)	979	7,691
Eliminate fossil-fuel tax preferences:		
-Eliminate coal preferences	1,108	2,579
-Eliminate oil and gas preferences	22,867	43,612
Tax carried (profits) interest as ordinary income	10,086	14,807
Deny deduction for punitive damages	127	312
Repeal lower-of-cost-or-market inventory accounting method	5,489	8,168
Simplify the tax code	148	407
Reduce the tax gap and make reforms:		
- Expand information reporting	-3,255	-8,005
-Improve compliance by businesses	3,281	8,774
-Strengthen tax administration	104	263
-Expand penalties	138	327
Estate tax	7,510	19,539
Total	115,094	280,254

Source: Office of Management and Budget , *Budget of the United States Government, Fiscal Year 2012: Summary Tables*, Washington, DC, February 14, 2011, pp. 183-187, at http://www.whitehouse.gov/sites/default/files/omb/ budget/fy2012/assets/ tables.pdf.

End Notes

[1] U.S. Office of Management and Budget, *Budget of the United States Government, Fiscal Year 2012*, at http://www.whitehouse.gov/omb/budget.

[2] The tax-related proposals discussed in this report are listed in Table S-2 of the FY2012 budget. Ibid., pp. 183-187, at http://www.whitehouse.gov/sites/default/files/omb/budget/fy2012/ assets/tables.pdf

[3] For detailed information see CRS Report RS21352, *The Earned Income Tax Credit (EITC): Changes for 2011 and 2012*, by Christine Scott.

[4] For more information about automatic enrollment in 401(k) plans see, CRS Report RS21954, *Automatic Enrollment in 401(k) Plans*, by John J. Topoleski.

[5] For more information about the AOTC and other tax benefits for higher education, see CRS Report RL32554, *An Overview of Tax Benefits for Higher Education Expenses*, by Mark P. Keightley.

[6] For detailed information, see CRS Report R40411, *The Economic Effects of Capital Gains Taxation*, by Thomas L. Hungerford and CRS Report RL31597, *The Taxation of Dividend Income: An Overview and Economic Analysis of the Issues*, by Jane G. Gravelle.

[7] For more information, see CRS Report RL31181, *Research Tax Credit: Current Law, Legislation in the 112th Congress, and Policy Issues* , by Gary Guenther

[8] For more information about the NMTC program, see CRS Report RL34402, *New Markets Tax Credit: An Introduction*, by Donald J. Marples.

[9] For more information about BABs, see CRS Report R40523, *Tax Credit Bonds: Overview and Analysis*, by Steven Maguire.

[10] Thomson-Reuters as provided by the Securities Industry and Financial Markets Association (SIFMA). Data available at http://www.sifma.org/research/statistics.aspx.

[11] For more information about the LIHTC program, see CRS Report RS22389, *An Introduction to the Design of the Low-Income Housing Tax Credit*, by Mark P. Keightley.

[12] The PAYGO baseline is intended to more accurately reflect the cost of tax proposals.

[13] For more information on the Superfund Trust Fund and the Superfund program, see CRS Report R41039, *Comprehensive Environmental Response, Compensation, and Liability Act: A Summary of Superfund Cleanup Authorities and Related Provisions of the Act*, by David M. Bearden.

[14] For more on the economics related to many of the reform proposals, see CRS Report R40623, *Tax Havens: International Tax Avoidance and Evasion*, by Jane G. Gravelle.

[15] For detailed information, see CRS Report RL32749, *U.S. Taxation of Overseas Investment and Income: Background and Issues*, by Donald J. Marples.

[16] For detailed information, see CRS Report RL32749, *U.S. Taxation of Overseas Investment and Income: Background and Issues*, by Donald J. Marples.

[17] For detailed information, see CRS Report RL31444, *Firms That Incorporate Abroad for Tax Purposes: Corporate "Inversions" and "Expatriation,"* by Donald J. Marples.

[18] The Pittsburgh Summit, "Leaders' Statement: The Pittsburgh Summit," press release, September 25, 2009, at http://www.pittsburghsummit.gov/documents/ organization/ 129853.pdf.

[19] The second method is cost depletion.

[20] The second method is cost depletion.

[21] Under current law the estate tax reverts to the pre-2001-2003 tax cuts level of $1 million in 2013. For budget scoring purposes, it is against this baseline that the cost of the provision is measured.

[22] Under current law, the estate tax exemption will drop to $1 million in 2013, the top rate reverts to 60%, the state death deduction reverts to a credit, and the portability option for spouses expires.

In: Federal Proposals for Tax Reform
Editors: S. G. Hannaford, E. Wallace
ISBN: 978-1-62257-960-0

Chapter 3

THE PRESIDENT'S FRAMEWORK FOR BUSINESS TAX REFORM*

The White House and Department of the Treasury

INTRODUCTION

America's system of business taxation is in need of reform. The United States has a relatively narrow corporate tax base compared to other countries—a tax base reduced by loopholes, tax expenditures, and tax planning. This is combined with a statutory corporate tax rate that will soon be the highest among advanced countries. As a result of this combination of a relatively narrow tax base and a high statutory tax rate, the U.S. tax system is uncompetitive and inefficient. The system distorts choices such as where to produce, what to invest in, how to finance a business, and what business form to use. And it does too little to encourage job creation and investment in the United States while allowing firms to benefit from incentives to locate production and shift profits overseas. The system is also too complicated—especially for America's small businesses. For these reasons, the President is committed to reform that will support the competitiveness of American businesses—large and small—and increase incentives to invest and hire in the United States by lowering rates, cutting tax expenditures, and reducing

* This is an edited, reformatted and augmented version of The White House and Department of the Treasury Joint Report dated February 2012.

complexity, while being fiscally responsible. This chapter presents the President's Framework for business tax reform. In laying out this Framework, the President recognizes that tax reform will take time, require work on a bipartisan basis, and benefit from additional feedback from stakeholders and experts. To start that process, this chapter outlines what the President believes should be five key elements of business tax reform.

President Obama's Five Elements of Business Tax Reform

1. Eliminate dozens of tax loopholes and subsidies, broaden the base and cut the corporate tax rate to spur growth in America: The Framework would eliminate dozens of different tax expenditures and fundamentally reform the business tax base to reduce distortions that hurt productivity and growth. It would reinvest these savings to lower the corporate tax rate to 28 percent, putting the United States in line with major competitor countries and encouraging greater investment in America.
2. Strengthen American manufacturing and innovation: The Framework would refocus the manufacturing deduction and use the savings to reduce the effective rate on manufacturing to no more than 25 percent, while encouraging greater research and development and the production of clean energy.
3. Strengthen the international tax system, including establishing a new minimum tax on foreign earnings, to encourage domestic investment: Our tax system should not give companies an incentive to locate production overseas or engage in accounting games to shift profits abroad, eroding the U.S. tax base. Introducing a minimum tax on foreign earnings would help address these problems and discourage a global race to the bottom in tax rates.
4. Simplify and cut taxes for America's small businesses: Tax reform should make tax filing simpler for small businesses and entrepreneurs so that they can focus on growing their businesses rather than filling out tax returns.
5. Restore fiscal responsibility and not add a dime to the deficit: Business tax reform should be fully paid for and lead to greater fiscal responsibility than our current business tax system by either eliminating or making permanent and fully paying for temporary tax provisions now in the tax code.

I. Cut Loopholes and Subsidies, Broaden the Base, and Cut the Corporate Tax Rate

The United States now essentially trades off greater tax expenditures, loopholes, and tax planning for a higher statutory corporate tax rate relative to other countries. This is a poor trade that produces a tax system that is uncompetitive relative to other countries, distorts business decision making, and slows economic growth.

In recent years, our major trading partners have overhauled their tax codes, lowered their statutory corporate tax rates, and in some cases broadened their tax bases. The United States has not enacted similar reforms, leaving the United States with the second highest statutory tax rate among advanced countries. In April 2012, after the scheduled reductions in Japanese tax rates go into effect, the United States will have the highest statutory corporate income tax rate in the Organization for Economic Cooperation and Development (OECD).

Figure 1 compares the statutory corporate tax rate in the United States to the GDP-weighted average rate in other OECD countries, including sub-national (such as state and local) corporate taxes where relevant. In 1986, the United States lowered its statutory tax rate to well below the average for other OECD countries. Since the late 1980s, however, many OECD countries have reduced statutory corporate tax rates so that the U.S. rate now exceeds the OECD average. In 2011, the U.S. statutory corporate income tax rate was 39.2 percent (including an average effective state and local combined rate of 4.2 percent in addition to the federal rate of 35 percent). That is over 11 percentage points higher than the weighted average statutory rate in other OECD countries (27.8 percent), almost 7 percentage points higher than the weighted average statutory rate in other G-7 countries (32.3 percent), and second only to Japan which is scheduled to lower its rate below the U.S. rate in April 2012 (see Table 1).[1]

The difference in statutory corporate tax rates between the United States and other advanced countries will further widen this year. For example, this year, the federal corporate income tax rate in Canada has decreased by 1.5 percentage points. In April, the United Kingdom is scheduled reduce its corporate tax rate by 1 percentage point, and, that same month, Japan will reduce its national corporate tax rate by 1.5 percentage points.

However, even as the United States has among the highest statutory corporate tax rates, the effective marginal tax rate on corporate investment in the United States is similar to that in other competitor countries (see Table 1). The effective marginal rate represents what businesses would actually expect to pay on a marginal investment. The discrepancy between where the United States ranks in terms of the statutory rate and in terms of the effective marginal rate comes about for a number of reasons. These include the United States having a narrower tax base—reduced by tax expenditures, loopholes, and tax planning—and the presence of other, higher taxes (such as property taxes) imposed on corporations in competitor countries. (For a full discussion comparing the U.S. statutory tax rate and average effective tax rate to those in other countries, see Appendix I.)

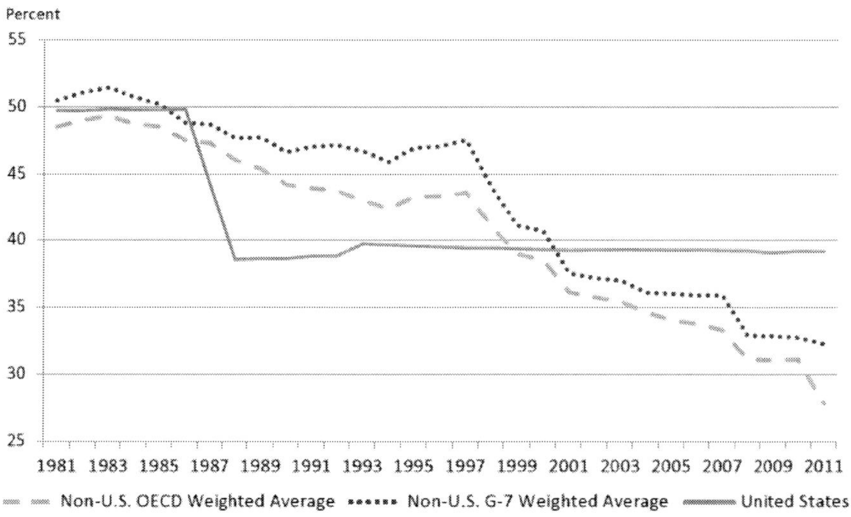

Figure 1. Comparison of Statutory Corporate Tax Rates in the United States and Oecd Countries.

While the United States is generally in line with competitor countries when it comes to the overall average level of taxes paid on corporate investments, this is not an argument against reform; in fact, it is an argument and motivation for reform. The trade-off of a higher statutory tax rate in exchange for a narrower tax base with numerous loopholes and subsidies is a poor one.

The tax preferences created by tax expenditures and loopholes add complexity to the tax system and contribute to a substantial business tax compliance burden. Additional rules and regulations are needed to limit incentives to their intended beneficiaries. Taxpayers have to spend time and money learning about tax incentives and often rely on third parties to help them navigate the thicket of complex tax rules. The Internal Revenue Service (IRS) has to spend resources monitoring and enforcing the rules. Disputes invariably arise between the IRS and taxpayers, and society expends resources adjudicating these disputes. In fact, it is estimated that the administrative and compliance costs in the corporate income tax system now exceed $40 billion per year, or more than 12 percent of revenue collected.[2]

Table 1. 2011 G-7 Statutory Corporate Tax Rates (in Percent)

Country	Statutory Corporate Tax Rate (including subnational taxes)	Effective Marginal Tax Rate (including subnational taxes)[b]
Canada	27.6	33.0
France	34.4	28.3
Germany	30.2	23.3
Italy	31.3	24.0
Japan	39.5	42.9
United Kingdom	26.0	32.3
United States	39.2	29.2
G-7 average excluding the U.S.[a]	32.3	31.9

[a] The G-7 Average is calculated using 2010 gross domestic product (in current US dollars) as weights. Source: OECD.

[b] See Table A1 in Appendix I for an explanation of the methodology for calculating the effective marginal tax rate.

Moreover, the tax expenditures and loopholes in the U.S. tax system, together with the structure of the corporate tax system, produce significant distortions that can result in a less efficient allocation of capital, reducing the productive capacity of the economy and U.S. living standards. The distortions created by the tax system are explored further below.

(i) Distorting the form of investment by industry and asset type

Currently, tax expenditures in the tax code vary dramatically by industry. These differences manifest themselves in disparate average tax rates across industries. Table 2 shows effective actual federal corporate tax rates by industry in 2007-2008. The overall average federal tax rate for U.S. corporations was 26 percent—well below the federal statutory rate of 35 percent. Within that average, there was considerable variation by industry—from a low of a 14 percent average tax rate for utilities to a 31 percent average tax rate for construction.[3]

Tax preferences also lead to very different effective marginal tax rates across assets. For example, because of accelerated depreciation and other features of the tax code, in 2005 income from a typical investment in structures for oil and gas faced an effective total marginal tax rate (including corporate and investor level taxes) of about 9 percent as compared to a 32 percent rate for manufacturing buildings.[4]

The result is a tax system that distorts investment decisions. By allocating capital inefficiently, this system lowers living standards now[5] and could also impede technological innovation. The pace of innovation is a key determinant of economic growth, and innovation tends to be directly related to those areas in which we make capital investments. Firms do not reap the benefits of technological advances until new capital is brought into production. Given this interplay between innovation and capital accumulation, the distortions created by the current corporate income tax may slow economic growth over the long term.

Table 2. Effective Actual Federal Corporate Tax Rates by Industry for 2007 – 2008

Industry	Effective Actual Corporate Tax Rate
Agriculture, Forestry, Fishing and Hunting	22%
Mining	18%
Utilities	14%
Construction	31%
Manufacturing	26%
Wholesale and Retail Trade	31%
Transportation and Warehousing	19%
Information	25%
Insurance	25%
Finance and Holding Companies	28%
Real Estate	23%
Leasing	18%
All Services	29%
Average Effective Actual Tax Rate	26%

Source: U.S. Department of the Treasury, Office of Tax Analysis.

(ii) Distorting the financing of investment

The current corporate tax code encourages corporations to finance themselves with debt rather than with equity. Specifically, under the current tax code, corporate dividends are not deductible from corporate taxable income, but interest payments are. This disparity creates a sizable wedge in the effective tax rates applied to returns from investments financed with equity versus debt. Profits generated by an equity-financed investment will be taxed at the 35 percent corporate rate, leaving 65 percent of the profits for dividend payments to shareholders. In contrast, profits from the same investment funded by debt will only be taxed to the extent they exceed the associated interest payments. Once the deductibility of interest is combined with accelerated depreciation, the cost of debt capital declines even further. In fact, on average, debt-financed investments are subsidized (i.e., their effective marginal tax rate is negative), as income generated by such investments is more than offset by deductions for interest and accelerated depreciation.

For example, the effective corporate marginal tax rate on new equity-financed investment in equipment is 37 percent in the United States. At the same time, the effective marginal tax rate on the same investment made with debt financing is *minus* 60 percent—a gap of 97 percentage points. This compares to an average difference of about 51 percentage points for other G-7 countries (see Table 3).[6]

This tax preference for debt financing has important macroeconomic consequences. First and foremost, outsized reliance on debt financing can increase the risk of financial distress and thus raise the likelihood of bankruptcy.

Unlike equity financing, which can flexibly absorb corporate losses, debt and the associated contractual covenants require ongoing payments of interest and principal and allow creditors to force a firm into bankruptcy. A solvent firm with limited liquidity that is struggling to make its debt payments may experience losses of customers, suppliers, and employees. It may engage in destructive asset "fire sales" and forgo economically profitable investments. And, in an attempt to avoid bankruptcy, levered firms faced with financial distress may resort to high-risk negative economic value investments.

In the broader context, a large bias towards debt financing in the corporate tax code may lead to greater aggregate leverage and the associated firm-level and macroeconomic costs of debt financing.[7]

Table 3. Effective Marginal Tax Rates for Debt and Equity Financed Corporate Investments: Selected Oecd Countries

Country	Effective Marginal Tax Rate Equipment (Equity)	Effective Marginal Tax Rate Equipment (Debt)	Difference
Australia	31	-23	-54
Austria	27	-14	-41
Belgium	5	-50	-55
Canada	28	-21	-49
Finland	27	-18	-45
France	29	-59	-88
Germany	32	-10	-42
Greece	14	-26	-40
Ireland	15	-4	-19
Italy	38	1	-37
Japan	49	-4	-53
Netherlands	27	-14	-41
Norway	33	-11	-43
Portugal	22	-34	-56
Spain	36	-22	-58
Sweden	24	-24	-48
Switzerland	22	-18	-40
UK	30	-9	-40
United States	37	-60	-97
Average, Excluding U.S. (unweighted)	34	-17	-51
G-7 Average, Excluding U.S. (unweighted)	37	-15	-51

Source: U.S. Department of Treasury, Office of Tax Analysis.

See notes to Table 1: G-7 Statutory and Effective Corporate Tax Rates (in Percent): 2011. Averages are calculated using 2010 gross domestic product (in current U.S. dollars) as weights

(III) Distorting the form of businesses

Business may be organized under a variety of different forms, including C-corporations, S-corporations, partnerships, and sole-proprietorships. These organizational forms offer varying legal, regulatory, and tax treatments. The primary difference in tax treatment between C-corporations, on the one hand, and S-corporations, partnerships, and sole-proprietorships, on the other, is applicability of the corporate income tax. C-corporations are subject to the corporate tax, while pass-through entities are not. (These other entities are known as "pass through" because profits pass through to the individual without being taxed at the entity level.)

The combined effect of this varying tax treatment has contributed to a lower effective tax rate for pass-through entities relative to C-corporations. The effective marginal tax rate on new investment by C-corporations is now 32.3 percent, while the effective marginal tax rate on new investment by pass-through businesses 26.4 percent.[8]

As a result, large companies are increasingly avoiding corporate tax liability by organizing themselves as pass-through businesses. Pass-through businesses represented less than one quarter of net business income in 1980, but more than 70 percent of net business income in 2008—the most recent year for which data are available (see Table 4).[9] While the pattern from year-to-year can be volatile, the overall trend is clear.

The ability of large pass-through entities to take advantage of preferential tax treatment has placed businesses organizing as C-corporations at a disadvantage. By allowing large pass-through entities preferential treatment, the tax code distorts choices of organizational form, which can lead to losses in economic efficiency; business managers should make choices about organizational form based on criteria other than tax treatment.[10]

IV. Distortions in favor of shifting production and profits overseas

A higher statutory rate can encourage corporations to shift income and production out of the United States to a lower tax jurisdiction, especially in today's global marketplace. The gain from shifting a dollar of income from one jurisdiction to another equals the difference in statutory tax rates between the two locations. The statutory rate may also affect the decision to invest in one country rather than another, especially where the investments are independent and highly profitable. This is particularly true for earnings and production that cannot benefit from special deductions and tax credits.

The empirical evidence suggests that income-shifting behavior by multinational corporations is a significant concern that should be addressed through tax reform.[11]

The pre-tax profitability of controlled foreign corporations is negatively correlated with local country statutory tax rates, taking into account real economic factors such as financial structure, capital employed, and other non-transfer pricing operational aspects of multinational groups.[12]

In addition to the evidence that companies generally shift income from high-tax foreign countries to low-tax foreign countries, there is also evidence of income shifting specifically from the United States to other countries.[13] Income shifting from the United States to other countries significantly erodes the U.S. tax base and leads to lower corporate tax receipts. Evidence suggests that high statutory tax rates may also affect a company's willingness to locate in the United States following mergers and acquisitions.[14]

Table 4. Shares of Total Business Returns, Receipts, and Net Income – 1980 to 2008

	1980	1990	2000	2008
S Corporations				
Returns	4%	8%	11%	13%
Total Receipts	3%	13%	15%	18%
Net Income (less deficit)	1%	10%	17%	22%
Partnerships [a]				
Returns	11%	8%	8%	10%
Total Receipts	4%	4%	10%	14%
Net Income (less deficit)	3%	4%	22%	32%
Sole Proprietorships				
Returns	69%	74%	72%	72%
Total Receipts	6%	6%	4%	4%
Net Income (less deficit)	18%	30%	18%	19%
C Corporations [b]				
Returns	17%	11%	9%	6%
Total Receipts	87%	77%	71%	64%
Net Income (less deficit)	78%	57%	43%	27%

[a] Includes LLC & LLPs

[b] Excludes 1120-RIC and 1120 REIT

Source: Internal Revenue Service, Statistics of Income, www.irs.gov/taxstats

President's Framework for Reform

The President's Framework would eliminate dozens of different tax expenditures and fundamentally reform the business tax base to reduce distortions that hurt productivity and growth. It would reinvest the savings in reducing the rate from 35 percent to 28 percent. This combination of a broader base and a lower rate would alleviate a number of the significant economic distortions identified above that cause businesses to base investment decisions on tax rules rather than economic returns. Furthermore, this would encourage greater investment here at home and reduce incentives for U.S. companies to move their operations abroad or to shift profits to lower-tax jurisdictions. Where appropriate, the changes would allow adequate transition periods to permit affected parties to adjust to the new permanent tax rules. Finally, this reform would bring certainty to a business tax code that annually features the expiration of dozens of business tax incentives. Many of these temporary provisions would be eliminated and those that remain would be made permanent—helping to improve incentives to allocate capital efficiently and to simplify the tax code.

Specifically, the President's Framework would:

- **Reduce the corporate tax rate from 35 percent to 28 percent**. This reduction in the rate would put the United States in line with other advanced countries, help encourage greater investment in the United States, and reduce the tax-related economic distortions discussed above.
- **Eliminate dozens of business tax loopholes and tax expenditures.** The President's plan would start from a presumption that we should eliminate all tax expenditures for specific industries, with the few exceptions that are critical to broader growth or fairness. The following are a few examples of specific reductions in tax expenditures and loophole closers that should be part of any reform:
  - *Eliminate "last in first out" accounting.* Under the "last-in, first-out" (LIFO) method of accounting for inventories, it is assumed that the cost of the items of inventory that are sold is equal to the cost of the items of inventory that were most recently purchased or produced. This allows some businesses to artificially lower their tax liability. The Framework would end LIFO, bringing us in line with international standards and simplifying the tax system.

- *Eliminate oil and gas tax preferences.* The tax code currently subsidizes oil and gas production through tax expenditures that provide preferences for these industries over others. The Framework would repeal tax preferences available for fossil fuels. This includes, for instance, repealing the expensing of intangible drilling costs, a provision that allows oil companies to immediately write-off these costs rather than recovering the cost over time as for most capital investments in other industries. This also includes repealing percentage depletion for oil and natural gas wells, which allows certain oil producers and royalty owners to recover the cost of oil and gas wells based on a percentage of the income they earn from selling oil and gas from the property rather than on the exhaustion of the property. Percentage depletion allows deductions that can exceed the cost of the property.
- *Reform treatment of insurance industry and products.* The tax code currently allows insurance to be used as a form of tax shelter for major corporations. In particular, corporations can invest in life insurance for their officers, directors, or employees, benefit from "inside build up" (gains on that investment) that are tax-deferred or never taxed, and finance that investment through debt that allows the corporation to take interest deductions earlier than any gain realized on the life insurance. The Framework would close this loophole and not allow interest deductions allocable to life insurance policies unless the contract is on an officer, director, or employee who is at least a 20 percent owner of the business. The Framework would also make a number of other reforms to the treatment of insurance companies and products to improve information reporting, simplify tax treatment, and close loopholes.
- *Taxing carried (profits) interests as ordinary income.* Currently, many hedge fund managers, private equity partners, and other managers in partnerships are able to pay a 15 percent capital gains rate on their labor income (on income that is known as "carried interest"). This tax loophole is inappropriate and allows these financial managers to pay a lower tax rate on their income than other workers. The Framework would eliminate the loophole for managers in investment services partnerships and tax carried interest at ordinary income rates.

- *Eliminate special depreciation rules for corporate purchases of aircraft.* This would eliminate the special depreciation rules that allow owners of non-commercial aircraft to depreciate their aircraft more quickly (over five years) than commercial aircraft (seven years).

- **Reform the corporate tax base to invest savings in cutting the tax rate and reducing harmful distortions.** This Framework lays out a menu of options that should be under consideration in reform. At least several of these would be necessary to get the rate down to 28 percent:
  - *Addressing depreciation schedules.* Current depreciation schedules generally overstate the true economic depreciation of assets. Although this provides an incentive to invest, it comes at the cost of higher tax rates for a given amount of revenue. In an increasingly global economy, accelerated depreciation may be a less effective way to increase investment and job creation than reinvesting the savings from moving towards economic depreciation into reducing tax rates.
  - *Reducing the bias toward debt financing.* A lower corporate tax rate by itself would automatically reduce but not eliminate the bias toward debt financing. Additional steps like reducing the deductibility of interest for corporations should be considered as part of a reform plan. This is because a tax system that is more neutral towards debt and equity will reduce incentives to overleverage and produce more stable business finances, especially in times of economic stress. In addition, reducing the deductibility of interest for corporations could finance lower tax rates and do more to encourage investment in the United States than keeping rates higher or paying for the rate reductions in other ways.
  - *Establishing greater parity between large corporations and large non-corporate counterparts.* Establishing greater parity between large corporations and their large non-corporate counterparts should be considered as a way to help improve equity, reduce distortions in how businesses organize themselves, and finance lower tax rates. A variety of ways to do this have been proposed, including ones discussed in the 2005 report of President Bush's Advisory Panel on Tax Reform,[15] and in reform options developed by President Obama's Economic Recovery Advisory

Board in 2010.[16] It is essential that any changes in this area should not affect small businesses.

- **Improve transparency and reduce accounting gimmicks.** Corporate tax reform should increase transparency and reduce the gap between book income, reported to shareholders, and taxable income, reported to the IRS. These reforms could include greater disclosure of annual corporate income tax payments.

II. Strengthen American Manufacturing and Innovation

The manufacturing sector plays an outsized role in the U.S. economy with significant spillovers to other sectors that make it particularly important to future job creation, innovation, and economic growth. Furthermore, the United States is in a global competition for manufacturing investment, and both existing and emerging manufacturing industries are subject to more intense international competition than other sectors.

Encouraging manufacturing investment and production supports higher wage jobs.[17] Manufacturing contributes disproportionately to U.S. innovation; manufacturing firms conduct more than two-thirds of the private sector research and development (R&D) in the United States and employ the majority of scientists and engineers in the private sector.[18] Investment in new production capacity and proximity to the manufacturing process create spillovers across firms and industries, leading to the ideas, capabilities, and technologies that enable innovation. In this way, investments in manufacturing increase innovation and economy-wide productivity growth.[19] In addition, manufacturing accounts for nearly 60 percent of total exports[20] and can help address our current account deficit. R&D is especially important for manufacturing, which is a technology-intensive sector. In the 1980s, the United States was the leader in providing tax incentives for R&D through the Research and Experimentation Tax Credit (R&E Tax Credit). Today, however, many nations provide far more generous tax incentives for research than does the United States. Current tax policy also undermines the effectiveness of the incentive for research, because it is extended periodically on only a temporary basis. Keeping this tax incentive under constant threat of expiration means that businesses planning for long-term research projects have to account for the risk that the credit will not be available, blunting its effectiveness as an incentive. The R&E Tax Credit has been extended temporarily 14 times since its creation in 1981, with some extensions lasting just 6 months. It was even allowed to lapse for 12 months in the mid-1990s, and, as of January 1, 2012, this tax credit had expired again.

Most studies based on historical and cross-country data find that the society-wide returns on R&D are much larger than private returns earned by the investors who fund R&D. Studies have found that social returns to R&D investment to be roughly twice the private returns,[21] a disparity which leads to private sector underinvestment in the absence of policies such as the R&E Tax Credit. The R&E Tax Credit is also a cost-effective policy for stimulating additional private sector investment. Most recent studies find that each dollar of foregone tax revenue through the R&E Tax Credit causes firms to invest at least a dollar in R&D, with some studies finding a benefit to cost ratio of 2 or 2.96.[22] Finally, this Framework recognizes that, as we expand manufacturing in the United States, the tax code should encourage doing so in way that is sustainable and that puts the United States in the lead in manufacturing the clean energy technologies of the future. This will create jobs here at home and can also have important spillover benefits. Moving toward a clean energy economy will reduce air and water pollution and enhance our national security by reducing dependence on oil. Cleaner energy will play a crucial role in slowing global climate change, meeting the President's goal of producing 80 percent of our nation's electricity from clean sources by 2035.

President's Framework for Reform

The Framework would strengthen America's manufacturing sector and encourage greater innovation. These are incentives that are important to growth and should have positive spillover effects across the economy. Specifically, the Framework would:

- Effectively cut the top corporate tax rate on manufacturing income to 25 percent and to an even lower rate for income from advanced manufacturing activities by reforming the domestic production activities deduction. Reflecting manufacturing's key role in innovation and the intense international competition facing the sector, the President's Framework would reform the current domestic production activities deduction. It would focus the deduction more on manufacturing activity, expand the deduction to 10.7 percent, and increase it even more for advanced manufacturing. This would effectively cut the top corporate tax rate for manufacturing income to 25 percent and even lower for advanced manufacturing.

- Expand, simplify and make permanent the R&E Tax Credit. Currently, businesses must choose between using a complex formula for calculating their R&E Tax Credit that provides a 20 percent credit rate for investments over a certain base and a much simpler one that provides a 14 percent credit in excess of a base amount. The complex formula is so outdated that it takes into account the amount of a business's R&D expenses from 1984 to 1988. The President's Framework would increase the rate of the simpler credit to 17 percent, which would make it more attractive and simplify tax filing for businesses. In addition, the credit would be made permanent to increase certainty and effectiveness.
- Extend, consolidate, and enhance key tax incentives to encourage investment in clean energy. The President's Framework would make permanent the tax credit for the production of renewable electricity, in order to provide a strong, consistent incentive to encourage investments in renewable energy technologies like wind and solar. As with the R&E Tax Credit, the United States has to date provided only a temporary production tax credit for renewable electricity generation. This approach has created an uncertain investment climate, undermined the effectiveness of our tax expenditures, and hindered the development of a clean energy sector in the United States. In addition, the structure of renewable production and investment tax credits has required many firms to invest in inefficient tax planning through tax equity structures so that they can benefit even when they do not have tax liability in a given year because of a lack of taxable income. The President's Framework would address this issue by making the permanent production tax credit refundable.

III. Strengthen the International Tax System to Encourage Domestic Investment

The international provisions of the corporate tax code create opportunities for U.S. companies to reduce their taxes by locating their operations and profits abroad. The tax system is subject to gaming, as corporations manipulate complex tax rules to minimize taxes and, in some cases, shift profit actually earned in the United States to low-tax jurisdictions.

The current U.S. tax system subjects foreign subsidiaries of U.S.-based multinationals to taxes on their overseas income (while allowing a tax credit for foreign taxes paid). However, often corporations do not need to pay taxes in the United States on that income until they repatriate it to the United States, a rule called deferral (since it defers taxation of the income). Many companies reinvest, rather than repatriate, a significant portion of their income overseas and as a result may never face U.S. taxes on much of that income. Although the U.S. tax system is often described as "worldwide" because it taxes U.S. companies on profits earned abroad, opportunities for deferral can make it effectively much closer to a territorial system—a system in which taxes are never paid on foreign income—for many companies.

Because of deferral, U.S. corporations have a significant opportunity to reduce overall taxes paid by shifting profits to low-tax jurisdictions—either by moving their operations and jobs there or by relying on accounting tools and current transfer pricing principles to shift profits there. There is ample evidence that U.S. multinationals' decisions about the choice of where to invest are sensitive to effective tax rates in foreign jurisdictions.[23] There is also strong evidence that corporations use accounting mechanisms to shift profits from where they are actually earned to tax havens and other low-tax jurisdictions.[24] Table 5 shows profits of U.S. corporations reported in select, small countries with very low tax rates. In a number of cases, the amount of profits far exceeds the country's actual output, suggesting the degree to which companies use these countries to shelter profits that may have been earned elsewhere.

Table 5. Select Small Countries – U.S. Foreign Company Profits Relative to GDP

Country	U.S. Foreign Company Profits Relative to GDP
Bahamas	43%
Bermuda	646%
British Virgin Islands	355%
Cayman Islands	547%
Jersey	35%
Liberia	61%
Marshall Islands	340%

Source: Jane G. Gravelle, Cong. Res. Service, Tax Havens: International Tax Avoidance and Evasion 14 Tbl.4 (2010).

This distortion in the tax system can lead to inefficient overinvestment abroad and underinvestment in the United States. It can also erode the U.S. tax base, requiring higher tax rates on income that remains taxable in the United States in order to collect the same amount of revenue. Finally, the international tax system is very complex, which not only burdens companies with complicated accounting and tax requirements, but also unfairly benefits the most sophisticated companies which are able to avoid paying taxes by manipulating intricate rules. There is considerable debate as to how to reform the international tax code. One proposal is to switch to a pure territorial system under which all active foreign income would either be taxed little or not at all in the United States. However, the Administration believes that a pure territorial system could aggravate, rather than ameliorate, many of the problems in the current tax code. If foreign earnings of U.S. multinational corporations are not taxed at all, these firms would have even greater incentives to locate operations abroad or use accounting mechanisms to shift profits out of the United States. Furthermore, such a system could exacerbate the continuing race to the bottom in international tax rates. At the same time, tax reform should be a foundation to maximize investment, growth and jobs in the United States. It should properly balance the need to reduce tax incentives to locate overseas with the need for U.S. companies to be able to compete overseas; some overseas investments and operations are necessary to serve and expand into foreign markets in ways that benefit U.S. jobs and economic growth. This will be a difficult and complex undertaking, but one guided by the sole criteria of promoting growth in the jobs and standard of living of American workers and their families.

President's Framework for Reform

The President proposes to protect the U.S. tax base and strengthen the international corporate tax system by establishing a new minimum tax on foreign earnings—while repealing deductions for shipping jobs overseas and providing new incentives for bringing jobs back home. Under the President's Framework, reform would:

- **Require companies to pay a minimum tax on overseas profits.** The President believes we must prevent companies from reaping the benefits of locating profits in low-tax countries, put the United States on a more level playing field with our international competitors, and help end the race to the bottom in corporate tax rates.

Specifically, under the President's proposal, income earned by subsidiaries of U.S. corporations operating abroad must be subject to a minimum rate of tax. This would stop our tax system from generously rewarding companies for moving profits offshore. Thus, foreign income deferred in a low-tax jurisdiction would be subject to immediate U.S. taxation up to the minimum tax rate with a foreign tax credit allowed for income taxes on that income paid to the host country. This minimum tax would be designed to balance the need to stop rewarding tax havens and to prevent a race to the bottom with the goal of keeping U.S. companies on a level playing field with competitors when engaged in activities which, by necessity, must occur in a foreign country.

- **Remove tax deductions for moving productions overseas and provide new incentives for bringing production back to the United States.** The tax code currently allows companies moving operations overseas to deduct their moving expenses—and reduce their taxes in the United States as a result. The President is proposing that companies will no longer be allowed to claim tax deductions for moving their operations abroad. At the same time, to help bring jobs home, the President is proposing to give a 20 percent income tax credit for the expenses of moving operations back into the United States.
- **Other reforms to reduce incentives to shift income and assets overseas**. The Framework would also clean up the international tax code and reduce incentives and opportunities to shift income and assets overseas. For example, as noted above, U.S. companies may use accounting rules or aggressive transfer pricing to shift profit offshore. This is particularly true in the case of profits associated with intangible assets (assets like intellectual property). The Framework would strengthen the international tax rules by taxing currently the excess profits associated with shifting intangibles to low tax jurisdictions. In addition, under current law, U.S. businesses that borrow money and invest overseas can claim the interest they pay as a business expense and take an immediate deduction to reduce their U.S. taxes, even if they pay little or no U.S. taxes on their overseas investment. The Framework would eliminate this tax advantage by requiring that the deduction for the interest expense attributable to

overseas investment be delayed until the related income is taxed in the United States.

IV. Simplify and Cut Taxes for America's Small Businesses

America's small businesses face a tax code that is unduly complex. Often, these firms—unlike large businesses—are not engaged in complex transactions, and yet they must spend significant time and resources trying to comply with the tax code. Small businesses are disproportionately burdened with tax compliance, and the cost of this burden is substantial. In 2004, small businesses devoted between 1.7 and 1.8 billion hours and spent between $15 and $16 billion on tax compliance. On average, each small business devoted about 240 hours complying with the tax code, and spent over $2,000 in tax compliance costs. An overwhelming share of the time burden is due to recordkeeping, while most of the money burden is spent on compensation for paid tax preparers.[25]

For some small businesses, the cost of tax compliance is particularly burdensome. In 2004, 9.7 percent of small business spent over $5,000 in tax compliance and 11.2 percent devoted in excess of 500 hours to compliance. Moreover, for very small businesses, the burden of tax compliance can approach the total amount of taxes paid. For example, for small businesses with between $10,000 and $20,000 in annual receipts, the money burden of compliance is between 6.8 and 7.8 percent of receipts while the time burden amounts to about half—between 51.9 and 52.9 percent—of total receipts. For small business owners with receipts of over $500,000, the average total burden—including the money and time burden—amounted to under 3 percent of total receipts.[26] The high compliance cost for small businesses is a drag on innovation and entrepreneurship. The large outlays for tax preparers means that small business owners have less capital to reinvest in their companies. The large amount of time spent on recordkeeping and understanding tax provisions means that small business owners have less time and energy for innovation and business development. There are other costs to complexity as well. Frustration with the tax code may eventually lead to weakened compliance and a higher gap between tax revenue owed and tax revenue paid. Moreover, complexity weakens the ability of tax policy to achieve its intended purpose. For example, small business owners might not take advantage of temporary investment incentives—such as the President's proposed expansion of section 179 expensing provisions—if they feel the tax code is too complex to understand overall.

President's Framework for Reform

Tax reform should make tax filing simpler for small businesses and entrepreneurs so that they can focus on growing their businesses rather than filling out tax returns. While some of the base-broadening provisions and other reforms described above would apply to both C-corporations and pass-through entities, the President's Framework includes provisions so that small businesses, including small pass-throughs, receive a net tax cut from reform.

As a way to reduce the tax code's complexity for small businesses and also provide small businesses with tax relief that on net more than offsets any of the base broadening reforms that would otherwise affect them, the President's Framework would:

- **Allow small businesses to expense up to $1 million in investments.** Since taking office, the President has secured enactment of temporary increases in the amount of qualified investments that small businesses can expense from $125,000 to $500,000—and, for 2011, temporarily increased that amount to 100 percent of qualified investments with no limit. Under the President's Framework, small businesses would, on a permanent basis, be allowed to expense up to $1,000,000 of qualified investments, which helps offset other changes to the tax base in reform that would affect small businesses. This would provide significant tax relief to America's small businesses and would allow small businesses to avoid the complexity of tracking depreciation schedules.
- **Allow cash accounting on businesses with up to $10 million in gross receipts.** Small businesses with up to $5 million in gross receipts are currently allowed to use this simplified form of accounting. Under the President's Framework, this threshold would increase to $10 million. This simplifies taxes for many more of America's small businesses, since cash accounting can be much easier than accrual accounting—which requires businesses to immediately recognize for income tax purposes their future cash receipts and costs.

In the Budget, the President has also proposed a number of discrete reforms that simplify the tax code for small businesses and provide them with tax relief—and that Congress could act on immediately and should also be included in any fundamental reform. These would:

- **Double the deduction for start-up costs**. This would double the amount of start-up expenses entrepreneurs can immediately deduct from their taxes from $5,000 to $10,000. This offers an immediate incentive for investing in starting up new small businesses, and it also simplifies accounting for small businesses, which must otherwise write off start-up expenses over a period of 15 years.
- **Reform and expand the health insurance tax credit for small businesses.** This credit, created in the Affordable Care Act, helps small businesses afford the cost of health insurance. This reform would allow small businesses with up to 50 workers to qualify for the credit (up from 25), provide a more generous phase-out schedule, and substantially simplify and streamline the tax credit's rules.

V. Restore Fiscal Responsibility

The Federal budget is on an unsustainable course. Even as the economy recovers, the United States carries the legacy of past policies that were not paid for at the time and will continue to drive deficits and debt in the future. Restoring fiscal responsibility will require a set of hard choices to constrain spending, while still making the investments we need in our future. Fiscal responsibility also requires that revenue be increased as part of a balanced approach that asks the wealthiest to contribute more, while protecting the middle class from tax increases. Given the fiscal outlook and the hard choices it requires, the business sector must also be asked to contribute to restoring fiscal sustainability.

President's Framework for Reform

Business tax reform should be fully paid for and be more fiscally responsible than our current system. Under the President's Framework, temporary business tax provisions that are continually extended and have been deficit-financed in the past would either be eliminated or, if they are continued and made permanent, such as the R&E Tax Credit, would be fully paid for within business tax reform. As a result, continuing these items— which, together, represent about $250 billion in costs over the next decade—would no longer add to the deficit under the President's Framework. In fact, the President's balanced approach to restoring fiscal sustainability should improve the investment environment in the United States by helping to keep interest rates low in the years ahead and limiting the crowding out of private investment by government borrowing once the economy recovers.

While a number of the measures that raise revenue in corporate reform—most consequentially, ending accelerated depreciation—raise more revenue in earlier years than they do in later years, the President is committed to corporate tax reform that does not add a dime to the deficit, over the next decade or thereafter. Put simply, the President will only accept business tax reform that is fiscally responsible.

APPENDIX I: STATUTORY TAX RATE VERSUS EFFECTIVE TAX RATE IN THE UNITED STATES

The statutory corporate income tax rate offers an incomplete description of investment incentives. The size of the tax base (e.g., the magnitude of depreciation deductions, interest deductions, and special preferences) also matters, as do certain other taxes that corporations must pay, such as property taxes in some countries. A more comprehensive summary measure of the tax burden would include a host of relevant tax rates, deductions, and credits. These more comprehensive measures suggest that the U.S. tax system is more in line with that of our major competitors in terms of effective tax rates, as opposed to a comparison based on statutory corporate income tax rates alone.

One such measure is the effective marginal corporate tax rate (EMTR). The EMTR is the hypothetical corporate tax rate that, if applied to economic income, would offer the same investment incentive on a new, just barely profitable, investment, as does the combination of tax rates, depreciation deductions, interest deductions, and, in some cases, other features that characterize the actual tax system. Generally, the lower the EMTR, the greater the incentive to invest.

The second column of Table A1 shows the EMTR in G-7 countries, including the United States. The calculations are for a representative mix of physical assets (equipment, buildings, and inventory), financed using a combination of debt and equity.

The United States' EMTR is close to, and actually is slightly below, the average for the other G-7 countries, despite the United States' relatively high statutory corporate income tax rate. Two factors largely account for this difference. One factor is the relatively high property and wealth taxes that are imposed by other G-7 countries. The second is debt finance and the value of the interest deduction.

The high statutory tax rate in the United States combined with a full deduction of nominal interest results in a very low EMTR on U.S. debt-financed investment. In contrast, the interest deduction does less to lower the EMTR in other countries, which tend to have lower statutory corporate income tax rates and some of which restrict the deductibility of interest.

The effective average corporate tax rate (EATR) is an alternative summary measure of the effect of taxes on investment incentives. This measure is a weighted combination of the EMTR and the statutory corporate income tax rate. It is intended to better capture investment incentives for lumpy, large, discrete investments, often involving intangibles such as patents and trademarks, on which firms might expect to earn pure profits, rather than just the normal return.

On such profitable investments, tax incentives such as accelerated depreciation, do not matter, while the statutory tax rate has a large effect. To the extent that the investment under consideration is a mix of assets earning pure profits and assets earning a normal return, the EATR can be relevant for measuring investment incentives. Because such investments—e.g., a factory designed to manufacture a product based on a patent—may be typical for a multinational corporation, the EATR frequently is used as a measure of the tax incentives that affect firms' decisions on where to locate investments.[27] In contrast, the EMTR is regarded as an appropriate measure of the effect of taxes on the decision about how big to make a factory in a given country, conditional on deciding to build the factory in that country.

The United States has an EATR that is somewhat above that for most other G-7 countries. This reflects the importance of the statutory corporate income tax rate (including subnational tax rates and surcharges) in the calculations. Nonetheless, because of the United States's relatively low EMTR, the United States is closer to the G-7 mean when considering EATRs than when looking at statutory corporate income tax rates alone.

Table A1. G-7 Statutory and Effective Corporate Tax Rates (in Percent) for 2011

	Statutory Corporate Tax Rate[c]	Overall Effective Tax Rates (Corporate Level)	
		Effective Marginal Tax Rate[b]	Effective Average Tax Rate[b]
Canada	27.6	33.0	29.6
France	34.4	28.3	32.3
Germany	30.2	23.3	27.9
Italy	31.3	24.0	28.9
Japan	39.5	42.9	41.0
United Kingdom	26.0	32.3	28.3
United States[d]	39.2	29.2	35.7
G-7 Average excluding the U.S.[a]	32.3	31.9	32.6

Source: U.S. Department of the Treasury, Office of Tax Analysis.

Notes: EMTR = effective marginal tax rates; EATR = effective average tax rates.

[a] The G-7 Average is calculated using 2010 gross domestic product (in current US dollars) as weights.

[b] The overall EMTR is calculated as the difference between an average cost of capital (across type of asset and type of finance) and an after-tax real rate of return. In calculating an average cost of capital across type of finance, Devereux, et al. (2009) use weights of 65 percent for retained earnings and new equity combined, and 35 percent for debt.

[c] Effective statutory corporate tax rates are obtained using tax parameters from Section A of Devereux, et al. (2009), "Project for the EU Commission, Effective Tax Levels Using the Devereux/Griffith Methodology," TAXUD/2008/CC/099, Report 2009, available at http://ec.europa.eu/taxation customs/resources/documents/publications/studies/etr company.pdf. The tax parameters used to calculate the effective statutory corporate tax rates are supplemented with data from the OECD Tax Database. The tax parameters used to calculate the PV of depreciation are supplemented with data from the PricewaterhouseCoopers Worldwide Tax Summaries and the International Bureau of Fiscal Documentation online.

[d] EMTRs and EATRs for machinery do not reflect the 100-percent bonus depreciation for property placed in service after September 8, 2010 and before January 1, 2012.

The effective statutory corporate tax rates include top statutory corporate income tax rates, surcharges, and local profits tax rates (nominal). The EMTR and EATR also include effective real estate tax rates and net wealth tax rates. The same real rate of return, inflation rate, and economic depreciation rates are used for all countries. As a result, any differences in EMTR and EATR reflect differences in tax regimes.

In sum, the analysis of EMTRs and EATRs suggests that the U.S. tax system offers investment incentives that are within the range of those offered by other G-7 countries.

Note that, as explained above in Section II, this does not argue against the need for base broadening, rate reducing tax reform. Using tax expenditures and tax incentives to lower the effective rate can be a less effective way at promoting efficient investment in the United States than a broader base with a lower rate. In this regard, when it comes to the EMTR and EATR, analysis shows that U.S. taxes are lower on investments that just break even (as measured by the EMTR) than on more profitable investments (as measured by the EATR). Corporate reform that broadened the tax base while simultaneously cutting the statutory corporate tax rate could be broadly consistent with maintaining the current U.S. EMTR, while reducing the EATR. As explained earlier, the EATR is often considered to reflect the effect of taxes on the location of an investment, while the EMTR is considered an indicator of the effect of taxes on the scale of an investment. Thus, in addition to the benefits already discussed in Section II of broadening the tax base, tax reform could, in this way, be effective in attracting highly profitable investment projects to the United States.

APPENDIX II: EFFECTIVE MARGINAL TAX RATES INCLUDING INDIVIDUAL INCOME TAXES

Other tables in this paper show effective tax rates at the corporate level. They do not include individual income taxes. Table A2 below also includes individual income taxes, and, with that included, the same biases discussed earlier in this paper remain. Marginal tax rates vary significantly by asset type, organizational type, and source of financing.

Table A2. Effective Marginal Tax Rates on New Investment (in Percent)
(Including Corporate Income Tax and Individual Income Tax)

Entity	Current-law Baseline
Business	30.1
Corporate Business	32.3
Asset Type	
Equipment[a]	27.3
Structures[b]	32.7

Entity	Current-law Baseline
Land[c]	39.0
Inventories[c,d]	41.9
Intangibles[e]	6.2
Financing	
Debt-financed	-4.4
Equity-financed	36.8
Noncorporate Business	26.4
Asset Type	
Equipment[a]	18.7
Structures[b]	24.6
Land[c]	30.6
Inventories[c,d]	33.8
Intangibles[e]	-3.1
Owner-occupied Housing	-3.5
Economy-wide	21.3

Source: U.S. Department of the Treasury, Office of Tax Analysis

The effective marginal tax rates (EMTR) shown combine the statutory corporate income tax rate, accelerated tax depreciation, the business interest deduction, the home mortgage interest deduction, and various individual-level taxes (including a noncorporate business income tax rate). The individual-level taxes are an average of 2013-2022 income-weighted federal marginal tax rates from Treasury's

Individual Tax Model. They are consistent with a current-law baseline, implying that they assume the expiration in 2012 of recently extended provisions of the 2001 and 2003 tax acts. Those provisions include lower marginal tax rates on ordinary income, preferential tax rates on capital gains and dividend income, an increase in the child tax credit, and marriage penalty relief.

[a] Includes both nonresidential and residential equipment.

[b] Includes nonresidential, tenant-occupied, and owner-occupied structures.

[c] The economic depreciation rate is set to zero and no tax depreciation is included when calculating effective marginal tax rates for land and inventories.

[d] For inventories, the real before-tax rate of return is a weighted average of the cost of capital under last-in-first-out (LIFO) accounting and first-in-first-out (FIFO) accounting.

[e] The intangible assets include research and development capital.

End Notes

1 The U.S. statutory corporate tax rate does not reflect the domestic production activities deduction, which effectively provides a lower rate for corporations with qualifying activities. This deduction is discussed in more detail below.

[2] PRESIDENT'S ECONOMIC RECOVERY ADVISORY BOARD, REPORT ON TAX REFORM OPTIONS: SIMPLIFICATION, COMPLIANCE, AND CORPORATE TAXATION 65 (2010). In a review of the literature, the Government Accountability Office makes a similar finding. GAO describes two studies that find that the cost of compliance for all businesses (corporations and partnerships) was $40 billion to $80 billion per year as of the early 2000s. GOV'T ACCOUNTABILITY OFFICE, GAO-05-878, SUMMARY OF ESTIMATES OF THE COSTS OF THE FEDERAL TAX SYSTEM 14 tbl.3 (2005).

[3] Calculations of the Treasury Office of Tax Analysis.

[4] CONG. BUDGET OFFICE, TAXING CAPITAL INCOME: EFFECTIVE RATES AND APPROACHES TO REFORM 10-11 tbl.2 (2005).

[5] *See, e.g.*, Alan J. Auerbach and Kevin Hassett, *Tax Policy and Business Fixed Investment in the United States*, 47 J. Pub. Econ. 141 (1992); Dale W. Jorgenson and Kun-Young Yun, *Tax Policy and Capital Allocation*, 88 SCANDINAVIAN J. ECON. 355 (1986).

[6] Calculations of the Treasury Office of Tax Analysis.

[7] *See, e.g.*, RUUD A. DE MOOJ, INT'L MONETARY FUND, TAX BIASES TO DEBT FINANCE: ASSESSING THE PROBLEM, FINDING SOLUTIONS (2011); Joel Slemrod, *Lessons for Tax Policy in the Great Recession*, 62 NAT'L TAX J. 387 (2009).

[8] Calculations of the Treasury Office of Tax Analysis.

[9] Internal Revenue Service, Statistics of Income, *available at* www.irs.gov/taxstats.

[10] *See, e.g.*, Austan Goolsbee, *The Impact Of The Corporate Income Tax: Evidence From State Organizational Form Data*, 88 J. PUB. ECON. 2283 (2004); Jeffrey K. Mackie-Mason and Roger H. Gordon, *How Much Do Taxes Discourage Incorporation?* 52 J. FIN. 477 (1997); Roger H. Gordon, and Jeffrey Mackie-Mason, *Tax Distortions to the Choice of Organizational Form*, 55 J. PUB. ECON. 279 (1994).

[11] *See, e.g.*, Eric J. Bartelsmana and Roel M.W.J. Beetsma, Why Pay More? Corporate Tax Avoidance Through Transfer
Pricing in OECD Countries, 87 J. PUB. ECON 2225 (2003); Edward D. Kleinbard, *Stateless Income*, 11 FLA. TAX REV. 699 (2011).

[12] See, for example, the review of the literature in DEPT. OF THE TREAS., REPORT TO THE CONGRESS ON EARNINGS STRIPPING, TRANSFER PRICING AND U.S. INCOME TAX TREATIES ch.3 (2007) and Jane Gravelle, *Tax Havens: International Tax Avoidance and Evasion*, 62 NATIONAL TAX JOURNAL 727 (2009).

[13] Harry Grubert, *Foreign Taxes and the Growing Share of Multinational Company Income Abroad: Profits, Not Sales, Are Being Globalized*, NAT'L TAX J. (forthcoming 2012).

[14] Harry Huizinga and Johannes Voget, *International Taxation and the Direction and Volume of Cross Border M&A*, 64 J. FIN. 1217 (2009).

[15] PRESIDENT'S ADVISORY PANEL ON TAX REFORM, SIMPLE, FAIR, AND PRO-GROWTH: PROPOSALS TO FIX AMERICA'S TAX SYSTEM 129 (2005).

[16] PRESIDENT'S ECONOMIC RECOVERY ADVISORY BOARD, *supra* note 2, at 74-77.

[17] For further discussion on the role of tradable sectors and their impact on unemployment and higher-wage jobs, see Michael Spence, *The Impact of Globalization on Income and Employment: The Downside of Integrating Markets,* FOREIGN AFFAIRS, July – Aug. 2011, at 28.

[18] For a review of the U.S. manufacturing sector, see generally DEP'T OF COMMERCE, THE COMPETITIVENESS AND INNOVATION CAPACITY OF THE UNITED STATES (2012).

[19] See, for example, PRESIDENT'S COUNCIL OF ADVISORS ON SCIENCE AND TECHNOLOGY, ENSURING AMERICAN LEADERSHIP IN ADVANCED

MANUFACTURING (2011); P. Gary Pisano and Willy C. Shih, *Restoring American Competitiveness*, HARV. BUS. REV. July – Aug. 2009, at 2; Erica Fuchs and Randolph Kirchain, *Design for Location? The Impact of Manufacturing Off-Shore on Technology Competitiveness in the Optoelectronics Industry*, 56 Management Science 2323 (2010); Michael Greenstone, Rick Hornbeck and Enrico Moretti, *Identifying Agglomeration Spillovers: Evidence from Winners and Losers of Large Plant Openings*, 118 J. POL. ECON. 536 (2010).

[20] Bureau of Economic Analysis, U.S. International Trade in Goods and Services, *available at* http://www.bea.gov/international/.

[21] LAURA TYSON AND GREG LINDEN, CTR, FOR AM. PROGRESS, THE CORPORATE R&D TAX CREDIT AND U.S. INNOVATION AND COMPETITIVENESS 7 (2012).

[22] See Kenneth J. Klassen, Jeffrey A. Pittman, and Margaret P. Reed, *A Cross-National Comparison of R&D Expenditure Decisions: Tax Incentives and Financial Constraints*, 21 CONTEMPORARY ACCOUNTING RESEARCH 639 (2004); Bronwyn H. Hall, *R&D Tax Policy During the Eighties: Success or Failure?*, 7 TAX POL. & THE ECON. 1 (1993).

[23] *See, e.g.*, Rosanne Altshuler and Harry Grubert, *Taxpayer Responses to Competitive Tax Policies and Tax Policy Responses to Competitive Taxpayers: Recent Evidence*, 34 TAX NOTES INT'L 1349 (2004); Harry Grubert and John Mutti, *Taxes, Tariffs and Transfer Pricing in Multinational Corporation Decision Making*, 33 REV. ECON. AND STAT. 285 (1991).

[24] *See supra* notes 11 - 12 and accompanying text.

[25] Donald DeLuca et al., *Aggregate Estimates of Small Business Taxpayer Compliance Burden*, IRS RESEARCH BULLETIN, 2007, at 147.

[26] *Id.* The tax burden can also vary by industry, with small businesses in manufacturing, construction, and retail trade devoting more time to compliance than businesses in other industries.

[27] Others question the relevance of this measure because the source of the profit is not explicitly considered. If the source of the apparent profit is a risk premium, then it is not clear that taxes would impose any burden on it because the disincentive effect of the tax on the expected returns is offset by the tax's reduction in the variance in the return (reduction in the risk borne by the investor). *See* JANE G. GRAVELLE, CONG. RES. SERVICE, INTERNATIONAL CORPORATE TAX RATE COMPARISONS AND POLICY IMPLICATIONS (2011).

In: Federal Proposals for Tax Reform
Editors: S. G. Hannaford, E. Wallace
ISBN: 978-1-62257-960-0

Chapter 4

AN OVERVIEW AND COMPARISON OF SENATE PROPOSALS TO EXTEND THE "BUSH TAX CUTS": S. 3412 AND S. 3413*

Margot L. Crandall-Hollick

INTRODUCTION

Many of the provisions of the Economic Growth and Tax Relief Reconciliation Act of 2001 (EGTRRA; P.L. 107-16) and the Jobs Growth Tax Relief Reconciliation Act of 2003 (JGTRRA; P.L. 108-27), henceforth referred to as the Bush tax cuts, are scheduled to expire at the end of 2012. Two bills introduced in the Senate—S. 3412, the Middle Class Tax Cut Act, offered by Senator Reid and S. 3413, the Tax Hike Prevention Act, offered by Senator Hatch—propose to extend some or all of these tax cuts for one year through the end of 2013.[1] A bill introduced in the House—H.R. 8, the Job Protection and Recession Prevention Act of 2012—is virtually identical to S. 3413 except for its treatment of a business expensing provision. Media reports indicate that votes on these proposals are expected to occur before the August 2012 recess.[2]

This chapter is organized to first provide an overview of the Bush tax cuts, followed by brief summaries of S. 3412 and S. 3413, henceforth referred to as

---

* This is an edited, reformatted and augmented version of Congressional Research Service, Publication No. R42622, dated July 25, 2012.

the Reid and Hatch proposals, respectively. Revenue loss estimates of certain provisions of these bills are also included, as well as a brief summary of H.R. 8. In addition, detailed summary tables comparing the Reid and Hatch proposals—to each other and to current law—are provided. Finally, this chapter concludes with a brief overview of the current policy debate surrounding the partial or full extension of the Bush tax cuts.

OVERVIEW

The Bush tax cuts gradually reduced individual income and estate tax liabilities between 2002 and 2010.[3] These tax cuts were extended for 2011 and 2012 by the Tax Relief, Unemployment Insurance Reauthorization, and Job Creation Act of 2010 (P.L. 111-312), henceforth referred to as the 2010 Tax Act.

The Bush tax cuts lowered income taxes in a variety of ways, including by

- reducing marginal tax rates on ordinary income;
- reducing long-term capital gains tax rates and the tax rate on dividends;
- reducing and then repealing income limitations for personal exemptions and itemized deductions (often referred to as PEP and Pease, respectively);
- expanding tax credits, including the earned income tax credit (EITC), the child tax credit, the adoption tax credit, and the dependent care tax credit;
- reducing the marriage penalty by expanding for married couples the standard deduction, the 15% tax bracket and the income phase-out for the EITC; and
- modifying education tax incentives, including Coverdell education saving accounts (ESAs), the student loan interest deduction, and the tax treatment of certain scholarships and fellowships. The Bush tax cuts also created an exclusion for employer-provided educational assistance.

The Bush tax cuts also gradually reduced the estate tax between 2002 and 2009, with a full repeal of the estate tax in 2010.[4] The estate tax is a tax on the estate of a decedent, levied against and paid by the estate.[5] Under EGTRRA, the amount of an estate which was exempt from taxation gradually rose from

$1 million per decedent in 2002 to $3.5 million per decedent in 2009, while the top tax rate under the estate tax fell from 50% to 45% over the same time period. In 2010 there was no federal estate tax.

The 2010 Tax Act reinstated the estate tax, but raised the exemption level and lowered the tax rate in comparison to the estate tax in effect in 2009. Specifically, the exemption amount in 2011 was set at $5 million per decedent (adjusted for inflation, this amount equals $5,120,000 per decedent in 2012) and the top tax rate was set at 35%. The estate tax is scheduled to increase in 2013 under current law, with a $1 million per decedent exemption level and 55% top tax rate.

The Bush tax cuts also temporarily enacted the AMT patch which was then extended several more times, most recently by the 2010 Tax Act which extended the AMT patch for one year— 2011. The Alternative Minimum Tax, or AMT, was designed to ensure that higher-income taxpayers who owed little or no taxes under the regular income tax because they could claim tax preferences would still pay some tax.[6] Unlike the ordinary income tax however, key components of the AMT are not indexed to inflation. This means that *without* Congressional action to adjust the structure of the AMT, additional taxpayers will be subject to the AMT as a result of inflation.

The AMT patch is an increase in the amount of income exempt from the AMT. In 2011, the AMT-exemption amounts were $74,450 for married individuals filing joint returns and $48,450 for unmarried individuals. These exemption amounts revert to $45,000 for married individuals and $33,750 for unmarried individuals in 2012. In addition, an AMT patch generally also includes a provision which allows taxpayers to reduce their AMT by nonrefundable personal tax credits. In 2012, since under current law there is no AMT patch, most nonrefundable personal credits are no longer allowed against the AMT.

A Comparison of S. 3412 and S. 3413

While there are many similarities between the Reid and Hatch proposals, they also differ in several key ways. (A complete comparison of the two bills is included in **Table 1**.) Specifically:

- The Reid proposal would extend the Bush tax cuts for taxpayers with income below $200,000 for single filers, $225,0000 for head of household filers, and $250,000 for married joint filers for 2013.[7]

Taxpayers with income above these thresholds would be subject to higher marginal tax rates—36% and 39.6%—than are currently in effect. The Hatch proposal would extend all the Bush tax cuts for 2013. For a detailed example of marginal tax rates under these proposals, see **Table 2**.

- The Reid proposal would extend other temporary provisions for 2013 that were originally included in the American Recovery and Reinvestment Act of 2009 (ARRA; P.L. 111-5) and subsequently extended by the 2010 Tax Act. Specifically, the Reid proposal would extend ARRA provisions that expanded the refundability of the child tax credit, reduced the marriage penalty of the EITC, increased the EITC for families with three or more children, created a new higher education tax credit—the American Opportunity Tax Credit, and disregarded tax refunds and refundable credits in the administration of means-tested Federal programs. The Hatch proposal would not extend these provisions.
- The Reid proposal does not address the estate tax. Hence, under current law, the estate tax would revert to a $1 million exemption level per decedent and a top tax rate of 55%. The Hatch proposal would extend the 2010 Tax Act provisions of the estate tax—a $5 million exemption level per decedent and top tax rate of 35%—for 2013.
- The Reid proposal would extend the AMT patch for one year, 2012, while the Hatch proposal would extend the AMT patch for 2012 and 2013.
- The Reid proposal would extend enhanced Section 179 expensing amounts and threshold limits—$250,000 and $800,000, respectively—for 2013. The Hatch proposal would extend the 2010 and 2011 enhanced expensing amounts and threshold limits—$500,000 and $2 million, respectively—for 2013.
- Finally, the Hatch proposal would require the Senate Finance Committee to report tax reform legislation within 12 months with a top individual rate of 35%, a top corporate rate of 25% and a permanent repeal of the AMT. The Reid proposal would not include this requirement.

To provide additional context for these proposals, **Table 1** and **Table 2** also include the tax law in effect for 2012 (referred to as current policy) and the tax law scheduled to be in effect in 2013 (referred to as current law).

Budgetary Cost

The Joint Committee on Taxation estimates the revenue losses from the Reid proposal (S. 3412) to be $249.66 billion over the 10-year budgetary window (2013-2022), while a complete estimate of the revenue losses from the Hatch proposal (S. 3413) are not currently available. Hence, the revenue losses from these bills are not currently comparable. However, partial scores of certain aspects of these proposals have been estimated by JCT.[8] According to these estimates:

- Under the Reid proposal, the revenue losses from extending the EGTRRA and JGTRRA individual income tax provisions for 2013 are estimated to be $129.53 billion over the 10-year budgetary window of 2013 through 2022, while the equivalent revenue losses under the Hatch proposal are estimated to be $177.49 billion between 2013 through 2022.
- Under the Reid proposal, the revenue losses from extending temporary tax cut provisions included in ARRA for 2013 are estimated to be $27.22 billion over the 10-year budgetary window of 2013 through 2022. The Hatch proposal does not extend these provisions.
- Under the Reid proposal, the revenue losses from extending enhanced Section 179 expensing amounts and threshold limits are estimated to be $878 million over the 10-year budgetary window of 2013 through 2022, while the revenue losses from the Hatch proposal regarding enhanced Section 179 expensing amounts and threshold limits are not currently available.
- Under the Reid proposal, the revenue losses from extending the AMT patch *for one year—2012*—are estimated to be $92.04 billion over the 10-year budgetary window of 2013 through 2022. An estimate of the revenue losses of the Hatch proposal AMT patch provision—which would extend the AMT patch for 2012 and 2013—is currently unavailable. However, the revenue loss estimates from a similar proposal recently introduced in the House (see below) would result in an estimated $192.73 billion in revenue losses over the 10-year budgetary window of 2013 through 2022.
- The Reid proposal does not address the estate tax and hence there are no revenue losses under this proposal in comparison to current law, while the revenue losses from the Hatch proposal—which extend the

2011 and 2012 estate tax provisions for 2013—are estimated to be $177.46 billion over the 10-year budgetary window of 2013 through 2022.

House Legislative Proposals

On July 24, 2012, Chairman Camp introduced H.R. 8, the Job Protection and Recession Prevention Act of 2012, henceforth referred to as the Camp proposal. This legislation is virtually identical to the Hatch proposal, except for its treatment of Section 179 expensing. The Camp proposal sets the Section 179 expensing amounts and threshold limits at $100,000 and $400,000, respectively for 2013 (these levels are indexed for inflation and are estimated to be $127,000 and $510,000, respectively in 2013).

The Joint Committee on Taxation estimates this proposal would result in an estimated $403.15 billion of revenues losses over the 10-year budgetary window of 2013 through 2022, with $178.63 billion a result of extending the individual income tax provisions of the Bush tax cuts, $31.21 billion a result of extending the 2011-2012 estate tax provision, $192.73 billion a result of extending the AMT patch for two years, and $581 million as a result of the Section 179 expensing provision.[9]

Policy Debate[10]

Supporters and opponents of the Bush tax cuts generally evaluate the Bush tax cuts from different perspectives. Supporters of the tax cuts stress both their long-term and short-term economic benefits. Opponents often emphasize that the tax cuts are costly in terms of reduced revenues and that the benefits of this policy disproportionally accrue to the highest income taxpayers.

When the Bush tax cuts were originally proposed, proponents stressed that by reducing marginal tax rates, this policy would lessen some of the distortions taxes had on work, saving, and investment, ultimately boosting long-term growth. For example, by reducing marginal tax rates, individuals would have more take-home pay, theoretically incentivizing them to work more.

Table 1. Side by Side Comparison of the Senate Bush Tax Cut Proposals for 2013

<table>
<tr><th>Provision</th><th>Current Policy In Effect in 2012 (Bush Tax Cuts in Effect)</th><th>Hatch Proposal for 2013</th><th>Reid Proposal for 2013</th><th>Current Law In Effect in 2013 (Bush Tax Cuts Expired)</th></tr>
<tr><td></td><td colspan="4">Bush Tax Cuts (EGTRRA and JGTRRA) and Applicable ARRA Modifications</td></tr>
<tr><td>10% Tax Bracket</td><td>This tax bracket applies to a portion of taxable income that was, prior to the Bush Tax Cuts, subject to the 15% bracket.
For more detail, see Table 2.</td><td>Same as under the Scenario "Current Policy."
For more detail, see Table 2.</td><td>Same as under the Scenario "Current Policy."
For more detail, see Table 2.</td><td>This bracket expires and taxable income that was previously subject to the 10% rate will be subject to the 15% rate.
For more detail, see Table 2.</td></tr>
<tr><td>Tax Rates in Top Four Tax Brackets</td><td>35% | 33% | 28% | 25%
For more detail, see Table 2.</td><td>Same as under the Scenario "Current Policy." For more detail, see Table 2.</td><td>The 28% and 25% brackets would remain unchanged from "Current Policy." The 33% bracket would be in effect for taxpayers with AGI under $200,000 single filers, $225,000 head of household filers and $250,000 married joint filers. a Taxable income above this threshold and below the limit for the 36% threshold would be subject to the 36% rate Taxable income subject to 35% rate would now be subject to 39.6% rate
For more detail, see Table 2.</td><td>39.6% | 36% | 31% | 28%
For more detail, see Table 2.</td></tr>
</table>

Table 1. (Continued)

Provision	Current Policy In Effect in 2012 (Bush Tax Cuts in Effect)	Hatch Proposal for 2013	Reid Proposal for 2013	Current Law In Effect in 2013 (Bush Tax Cuts Expired)
Tax Rates on Capital Gains and Dividends	The top tax rate for both long-term capital gains and qualified dividends is 15%.	Same as under the Scenario "Current Policy."	The top tax rate for both long-term capital gains and qualified dividends remains 15% for taxpayers with AGI under the applicable threshold. The top tax rate for both long-term capital gains and qualified dividends would rise to 20% for taxpayers with AGI above the applicable threshold. The applicable threshold is \$200,000 for single filers, \$225,000 for head of household filers, and \$250,000 for married joint filers.[a]	The top tax rate for long-term capital gains will rise to 20% and dividends will be taxed at ordinary income tax rates. b
Limits on Itemized Deductions (Pease)	There are no income limitations on the overall amount of itemized deductions a taxpayer can claim (i.e., the Pease imitation is fully repealed).	Same as under the Scenario "Current Policy."	There will be no income limitations on the overall amount of itemized deductions for taxpayers with AGI below the applicable threshold.	The overall limitation on itemized deductions will be restored. For higher income taxpayers, the total amount of itemized deductions will be reduced by 3% of the amount by which the taxpayer's AGI exceeds an applicable threshold, adjusted annually for inflation.

Provision	Current Policy In Effect in 2012 (Bush Tax Cuts in Effect)	Hatch Proposal for 2013	Reid Proposal for 2013	Current Law In Effect in 2013 (Bush Tax Cuts Expired)
			The overall limitation on itemized deductions would be in effect for taxpayers with income above the applicable AGI threshold (i.e., the Pease imitation is partially repealed). The applicable threshold is $200,000 and $250,000 for married joint filers. a	The total amount of itemized deductions will not be reduced by more than 80%. For 2013, the JCT estimates the applicable Pease threshold to be $177,550.
Personal Exemptions Phase-Out (PEP)	There are no overall income restrictions on the amount of personal exemptions a taxpayer can claim (i.e., the PEP limitation is fully repealed).	Same as under the Scenario "Current Policy."	There will be no income limitations on the overall amount of personal exemptions for taxpayers with AGI below the applicable threshold. The overall limitation on personal exemptions would be in effect for taxpayers with income above the applicable AGI threshold (i.e., the PEP limitation is partially repealed). The applicable threshold is set at $200,000 for singles, $225,000 for head of household filers, and $250,000 for married joint filers. a	The limit on personal exemptions will be restored. For higher income taxpayers, the total amount of exemptions that can be claimed will be reduced by 2% for each $2,500 by which the taxpayer's AGI exceeds applicable thresholds, adjusted annually for inflation. For 2013, the JCT estimates the applicable Pease threshold to be $177,550 for single filers, $221,950 for head of household filers and $266,300 for married joint filers.

Table 1. (Continued)

Provision	Current Policy In Effect in 2012 (Bush Tax Cuts in Effect)	Hatch Proposal for 2013	Reid Proposal for 2013	Current Law In Effect in 2013 (Bush Tax Cuts Expired)
Child Tax Credit	The child credit is $1,000 per eligible child. The child tax credit is partially refundable using the earned income formula which is equal to 15% of a family's earnings in excess of a refundability threshold of $10,000 (indexed for inflation annually). ARRA Modifications ARRA lowered the refundability threshold used in the formula to $3,000 (not indexed for inflation) for 2009 and 2010. This lower threshold was extended for 2011 and 2012 by P.L. 111-312.	The proposal would extend the modifications made to the child tax credit by the Bush tax cuts. It would not extend the ARRA modifications.	Same as under the Scenario "Current Policy." Both the Bush tax cuts and the ARRA modifications would be extended.	The child credit will be $500 per eligible child. The child tax credit will be non-refundable for most families (the earned income formula expires).
Adoption Tax Benefits	Eligible taxpayers can claim two adoption tax benefits, although the combined level of qualified expenses is limited to $10,000 (indexed for inflation).	Same as under the Scenario "Current Policy."	Same as under the Scenario "Current Policy."	The adoption tax credit will be available only for special needs adoptions. The exclusion for employer provided adoption assistance will expire. The limit for the credit will be reduced to $6,000 (not indexed for inflation). The phase-out range for the credit will be $75,000-$115,000 (not indexed for inflation).

Provision	Current Policy In Effect in 2012 (Bush Tax Cuts in Effect)	Hatch Proposal for 2013	Reid Proposal for 2013	Current Law In Effect in 2013 (Bush Tax Cuts Expired)
	In 2012, this limit is $12,650. Specifically, in 2012, a taxpayer can either exclude from their income up to $12,650 of employer provided adoption assistance or claim a tax credit of up to $12,650, or a combination of both tax benefits as long as the combined level of qualified expenses does not exceed $12,650. In 2012, the combined limit for qualified expenses is $12,650. Both the tax credit and exclusion phase-out for taxpayers with incomes between $189,710-$229,710 in 2012 (indexed for annually for inflation).			
Dependent Care Tax Credit	The dependent care credit is equal to 35% of the first $3,000 of eligible expenses for one qualifying individual ($6,000 of qualifying expenses for two or more eligible individuals). The 35% credit rate is reduced for incomes above $15,000.	Same as under the Scenario "Current Policy."	Same as under the Scenario "Current Policy."	The dependent care credit will be equal to 30% of the first $2,400 of eligible expenses for one qualifying individual ($4,800 for two or more qualifying individuals). The 30% credit rate will be reduced for incomes above $10,000.

Table 1. (Continued)

Provision	Current Policy In Effect in 2012 (Bush Tax Cuts in Effect)	Hatch Proposal for 2013	Reid Proposal for 2013	Current Law In Effect in 2013 (Bush Tax Cuts Expired)
Standard Deduction for Married Couples	The deduction for married couples is 200% the deduction for singles	Same as under the Scenario "Current Policy."	Same as under the Scenario "Current Policy."	The deduction for married couples will be 167% the deduction for singles.
15% Bracket for Married Couples	The upper limit of this bracket is equal to 200% (i.e., double) the upper limit for singles.	Same as under the Scenario "Current Policy."	Same as under the Scenario "Current Policy."	The upper limit of this bracket will be equal to 167% of the upper limit for singles.
Earned Income Tax Credit Marriage Penalty Relief	The income level at which the EITC begins to phase-out for married taxpayers in comparison to unmarried taxpayers was increased. Specifically, it was increased by $3,000 under EGTRRA. ARRA Modifications This amount was increased to $5,000 by ARRA (this amount was indexed for inflation). This modification was extended for 2011 and 2012 by P.L. 111-312.	The proposal would extend the modifications made to the child tax credit by the Bush tax cuts. It would not extend the ARRA modifications. Hence, the phase-out level for married taxpayers would be $3,000 more than the level for unmarried taxpayers. (This increase in the phase-out level would be indexed for inflation.)	Same as under the Scenario "Current Law in 2012." Both the EGTRRA and ARRA modifications would be extended, hence the $5,000 increase in phase-out level would be extended. (This increase in the phase-out level would be indexed for inflation.)	The higher phase-out level for married taxpayers will expire and their phase-out levels will be the same as for unmarried taxpayers.
Employer Provided Educational Assistance	Up to $5,250 of qualifying employer provided educational assistance is excluded from income and hence not subject to taxation.	Same as under the Scenario "Current Policy."	Same as under the Scenario "Current Policy."	The provision will expire.

Provision	Current Policy In Effect in 2012 (Bush Tax Cuts in Effect)	Hatch Proposal for 2013	Reid Proposal for 2013	Current Law In Effect in 2013 (Bush Tax Cuts Expired)
Student Loan Interest Deduction	Up to $2,500 of student loan interest expenses can be deducted from gross income (as an above-the-line deduction). The amount that can be deducted phases out between $55,000-$70,000 for single filers and $110,000-$140,000 for married joint filers, adjusted for inflation.	Same as under the Scenario "Current Policy."	Same as under the Scenario "Current Policy."	The deduction can only be claimed by eligible taxpayers for the first 60 months (5 years) of interest payments. In addition, the income phase-out levels are reduced to $40,000-$55,000 for single filers and $60,000-$75,000 for married joint filers, adjusted for inflation.
Coverdells Education Savings Accounts (ESAs)	Coverdell ESAs are modified in several ways, including: (1) The maximum contribution amount for a beneficiary is $2,000 per year (2) Qualified expenses include elementary and secondary school expenses (kindergarten through 12th grade), in addition to higher education expenses (3) The phase-out range for married taxpayers is $190,000-$220,000, not indexed for inflation (double the phase-out range for singles) (4) Age limitations are waived for special needs beneficiaries	Same as under the Scenario "Current Policy."	Same as under the Scenario "Current Policy."	These modifications expire, hence: (1) The maximum contribution amount for a beneficiary will be $500 per year (2) Qualified expenses will be limited to higher education expenses (3) The phase-out range for marrie taxpayers will be $150,000-$160,000, not indexed for inflation (4) Contributions can be made up until the beneficiary is 18 years old and all distributions must be made when the beneficiary turns 30 for both non-special needs and special needs beneficiaries

Table 1. (Continued)

Provision	Current Policy In Effect in 2012 (Bush Tax Cuts in Effect)	Hatch Proposal for 2013	Reid Proposal for 2013	Current Law In Effect in 2013 (Bush Tax Cuts Expired)
	(5) Beneficiaries who use Coverdells can also claim education tax credits without penalty (expenses paid for with Coverdell funds cannot be used to claim credits) (6) Contributions can be made to both a 529 plan and Coverdell for the same beneficiary without penalty.			(5) If taxpayers claim education tax credits when they take a Coverdell distribution, their distribution will be subject to taxation (6) Contributions made to a Coverdell for a beneficiary will be subject to a 6% excise tax if contributions for the same beneficiary are made to a 529 plan in the same year.
Tax Treatment of National Health Service Corps Scholarships and F. Edward Herbert Armed Forces Health Professions Scholarship and Financial Assistance Programs	Students must generally pay taxes on any part of a scholarship, fellowship, or tuition reduction that can be attributed to teaching, research, or other services that have been performed, are being performed, or will be performed. A temporary exception to this general rule is allowed for funding received from the National Health Service Corps Scholarship Program and the F. Edward Hebert Armed Forces Health Professions Scholarship and Financial Assistance Program.	Same as under the Scenario "Current Policy."	Same as under the Scenario "Current Policy."	Funding received from the National Health Service Corps Scholarship Program and the F. Edward Hebert Armed Forces Health Professions Scholarship and Financial Assistance Program will be included as part of income and hence subject to taxation.

Provision	Current Policy In Effect in 2012 (Bush Tax Cuts in Effect)	Hatch Proposal for 2013	Reid Proposal for 2013	Current Law In Effect in 2013 (Bush Tax Cuts Expired)
Estate Tax Exemption Level and Top Rate	Under EGTRRA the estate tax gradually phased out such that in 2009, the top exemption amount was $3.5 million per decedent with a 45% tax rate and there was no estate tax in 2010. Per legislative changes made by P.L. 111-312 for 2011 and 2012, the exemption amount was equal to $5 million per decedent indexed for inflation and the top tax rate was 35%.	Same as under the Scenario "Current Policy. " Specifically the exemption amount would be $5 million per decedent indexed for inflation and the top tax rate would be 35%.	Same as under the Scenario "Current Law."	The top exemption amount will fall to $1 million per decedent (not indexed for inflation) and the top tax rate will rise to 55%.
Other Provisions				
AMT Patch	The AMT Patch expired at the end of 2011. Hence for the 2012 tax year, the AMT exemption amounts were $33,750 for individuals and $45,000 for married individuals in 2012. In 2012, under current law, most nonrefundable personal credits will no longer be allowed against the AMT.	The proposal reinstates the AMT Patch for 2012 and 2013. For 2012, the exemption amounts would be $50,600 for individuals and $78,750 for married joint filers. For 2013, the respective exemption amounts would be $51,150 and $79.850. Nonrefundable personal credit would be allowed against the AMT for 2012 and 2013.	The proposal reinstates the AMT Patch for 2012. For 2012, the exemption amounts would be $50,600 for individuals and $78,750 for married joint filers. Nonrefundable personal credit would be allowed against the AMT for 2012.	NA

Table 1. (Continued)

Provision	Current Policy In Effect in 2012 (Bush Tax Cuts in Effect)	Hatch Proposal for 2013	Reid Proposal for 2013	Current Law In Effect in 2013 (Bush Tax Cuts Expired)
EITC Expansion (ARRA)	The EITC for families with three or more children is 45% as a result of ARRA modifications.	Same as under the Scenario "Current Law."	Same as under the Scenario "Current Policy." The EITC expansion for families with three or more children would be extended.	The 45% EITC for families with three or more children will expire. Families with three or more children will be eligible for the 40% EITC (which is for families with two or more children).
The American Opportunity Tax Credit (AOTC)	The AOTC is in effect. The ARRA temporarily replaced the permanent Hope Credit for higher education expenses with the larger and partially refundable American Opportunity Tax Credit (AOTC), and P.L. 111-312 extended this credit for 2011 and 2012.	Same as under the Scenario "Current Law." The AOTC would expire.	Same as under the Scenario "Current Policy." The AOTC would be extended.	The AOTC will expire. Taxpayers may be eligible for the Hope Credit.
Section 179 Expensing	Taxpayers may elect to deduct the cost of a property placed in service for a given year instead of depreciating those costs over time. The amount that can be deducted and the income level at which this benefit phases out have been increased temporarily several times.	The maximum amount that could be deducted would be set at $500,000, with a $2 million phase-out level.	The maximum amount that could be deducted would be set at $250,000, with a $800,000 phase-out level.	In 2013, the temporary expansions to the section 179 deduction will expire and the parameters of the deduction will revert to their permanent levels. Specifically, the maximum amount that can be deducted will fall to $25,000, with a phase-out level of $200,000.

Provision	Current Policy In Effect in 2012 (Bush Tax Cuts in Effect)	Hatch Proposal for 2013	Reid Proposal for 2013	Current Law In Effect in 2013 (Bush Tax Cuts Expired)
	In 2012, the maximum amount that can be deducted is $125,000, with a phase-out level of $500,000.			
Disregard for Means Tested Programs	P.L. 111-312 included a provision which disregarded all refundable tax credits and refunds when determining eligibility for means tested programs in 2012.	The refund and tax credit disregard would expire.	The refund and tax credit disregard would be extended.	Refunds and tax credits will be included when determining eligibility for certain means-tested programs.

Sources: S. 3413 and S. 3412, The Joint Committee on Taxation. JCS-2-12; and Table 1 in CRS Report R42485, An Overview of Tax Provisions Expiring in 2012, by Margot L. Crandall-Hollick.

Notes: EGTRRA refers to the Economic Growth and Tax Relief Reconciliation Act of 2001 (P.L. 107-16) and JGTRRA refers to the Jobs Growth Tax Relief Reconciliation Act of 2003 (P.L. 108-27). There are other provisions addressed in the both the Hatch and Reid proposals, specifically (1) EGTRRA provided employers with a tax credit of up to $150,000 for acquiring, constructing, rehabilitating, or expanding property used for a child care facility. The Hatch and Reid proposals extend this provision for 2013; (2) EGTRRA increased the small-issuer arbitrage rebate exception for school construction from $10 million to $15 million. The Hatch and Reid proposals extend this $15 million level for 2013; (3) EGTRRA expanded the definition of private activity fog which tax-exempt bonds may be issued to include bonds for qualified public educational facilities. The Hatch and Reid proposals extend the allowance to issue tax-exempt private bonds for public school facilities for 2013; (4) EGTRRA allowed an election in which Alaska Native Settlement trusts can pay a lower tax rate than generally applies to trusts. The Hatch and Reid proposals extend the this tax relief for 2013.

NA = not applicable.

[a] These applicable thresholds are indexed for inflation occurring since 2009.

[b] In addition, a scheduled 3.8% surtax on investment income for taxpayers with income above the $200,000/$250,000 married joint filer threshold, included as part of the Affordable Care Act, is scheduled to go into effect in 2013.

Table 2. Tax Brackets Under S. 3413 and S. 3412 for Different Filing Statuses, 2013

Hatch Proposal-S. 3413 (Current Policy)		Current Law		Reid Proposal-S. 3412	
		Single Filers			
Taxable Income (over-but not over) $0-$8,900	Rate 10%	Taxable Income (over-but not over)	Rate	Taxable Income (over-but not over) $0-$8,900	Rate 10%
		$0-$36,150	15%		
$8,900-$36,150	15%			$8,900-$36,150	15%
$36,150-$87,550	25%	$36,150-$87,550	28%	$36,150-$87,550	25%
$87,550-$182,600	28%	$87,550-$182,600	31%	$87,550-$182,600	28%
				$182,600-$202.900 a	33%
$182,600-$397,000	33%	$182,600-$397,000	36%		
				$202,900a-$397,000	36%
$397,000-	35%	$397,000	39.6%	$397,000	39.6%
		Head of Household Filers			
Taxable Income (over-but not over)	Rate	Taxable Income (over-but not over)	Rate	Taxable Income (over-but not over)	Rate
$0-$12,700	10%			$0-$12,700	10%
		$0-$48,400	15%		
$12,700-$48,400	15%			$12,700-$48,400	15%
$48,400-$125,000	25%	$48,400-$125,000	28%	$48,400-$125,000	25%
$125,000-$202,450	28%	$125,000-$202,450	31%	$125,000-$202,450	28%
				$202,450-$224,550b	33%

Hatch Proposal-S. 3413 (Current Policy)		Current Law		Reid Proposal-S. 3412	
		Single Filers			
$202,450-$397,000	33%	$202,450-$397,000	36%		
				$224,550b-$397,000	36%
$397,000-	35%	$397,000	39.6%	$397,000	39.6%
		Married Joint Filers			
Taxable Income (over-but not over)	Rate	Taxable Income (over-but not over)	Rate	Taxable Income (over-but not over)	Rate
$0-$17,800	10%			$0-$17,800	10%
		$0-$63,500c	15%		
$17,800-$72,300c	15%			$17,800-$72,300c	15%
$72,300-$145,900	25%	$60,350-$145,900	28%	$72,300-$145,900	25%
$145,900-$222,300	28%	$145,900-$222,300	31%	$145,900-$222,300	28%
				$222,300-$246,200d	33%
$222,300-$397,000	33%	$222,300-$397,000	36%		
				$246,200d-$397,000	36%
$397,000-	35%	$397,000	39.6%	$397,000	39.6%

Source: Joint Committee on Taxation, Description of Revenue Provisions Contained In The President's Fiscal Year 2013 Budget Proposal, June 18, 2012, JCS-2-12, Tables 5 & 6.

Notes: These brackets are based on estimates of the individual income rate structure in 2013 from the Joint Committee on Taxation. The actual brackets for 2013 may differ.

[a] In 2013, the 33% bracket in effect in 2012 is split into the 33% and 36% bracket with single filers with taxable income less than $202,900 ($200,000 of AGI minus the basic standard deduction and one personal exemption, adjusted for inflation), subject to the 33% rate.

[b] In 2013, the 33% bracket in effect in 2012 is split into the 33% and 36% bracket. The starting point of the 36% bracket is set at the midpoint of the starting point for single filers and married joint filers, rounded down to the nearest $50.

[c] For married joint filers, the top of the 15% bracket is scheduled to be equal to 167% of the top of the 15% bracket for singles upon the extension of the Bush Tax Cuts. The extension of the Bush Tax Cuts would extend the provision whereby the 15% bracket for married joint filers is 200% the bracket for singles.

[d] In 2013, the 33% bracket in effect in 2012 is split into the 33% and 36% bracket with married joint filers with taxable income less than $246,200 ($250,000 of AGI minus the basic standard deduction and two personal exemptions, adjusted for inflation), subject to the 33% rate.

Advocates also highlighted that lower marginal rates on investment income—capital gains and dividends—would encourage increased investment, although analysis indicates capital gains may have little or no effect on saving.[11] Ultimately, this increased economic activity would boost longterm economic growth. The results of many economic studies, have shown that tax cuts generally do affect growth (and components of growth).[12] They have also generally shown, however, that the impact of tax cuts on growth is small in relation to the foregone revenue resulting from the cut.[13]

When the Bush tax cuts were being considered by Congress in 2001, the economy had slipped into a recession. Tax-cut advocates were highlighting the short-term stimulative benefits of the tax cuts. The scheduled expiration of the Bush tax cuts at the end of 2012 is also occurring at a time of relatively weak economic growth and high unemployment. Recent estimates by CBO have concluded that the extension of the Bush tax cuts would have a limited stimulative benefit on the economy in 2013—estimating that every $1 dollar of Bush tax cuts would result in 10 to 60 cents of additional GDP.[14] Yet, while the Bush tax cuts may not have been an effective short-term stimulus *in response to a recession*, some economists warn that allowing these tax cuts to expire in 2013, at the same time as a scheduled fiscal contraction, may have a negative effect on the economy.[15]

Opponents of extending all the Bush tax cuts highlight both their high cost as well as the fact that most of the benefits go to upper-income taxpayers. Recent estimates by CBO indicate that the Bush tax cuts, whose costs were not offset, increased the deficit by $1.75 trillion over the past 10 years (2002-2011).[16] The 2010 Tax Act's two-year extension of the income and estate tax provisions of the Bush tax cuts (including the ARRA modifications which are also proposed to be extended by the Reid proposal) reduced revenues by $475.79 billion over a 10-year budgetary window (2011-2020).[17] Of these revenue losses, $363.55 billion is attributable to the extension of the income tax provisions of EGTRRA and JGTRRA. However, the revenue losses of the extending the Bush tax cuts for all but high income taxpayers is significant. The Reid and Hatch proposals to extend the EGTRRA and JGTRRA individual income tax provisions for one year— 2013—would reduce revenues by $129.53 billion and $177.46 billion respectively for the 10-year budgetary window from 2013 through 2022.[18] Hence, extending the Bush tax cuts for taxpayers with income below $200,000 for single filers and $250,000 for married joint filers would cost approximately 72% of extending the tax cuts for all taxpayers.

While the expiration of the Bush tax cuts for higher income taxpayer may not yield significant cost savings in comparison to an extension for all taxpayers, critics still posit that it will help lessen inequity in the tax code that resulted from the Bush tax cuts. According to estimates examining tax burdens in 2010, the Bush tax cuts resulted in the lowest 20% of taxpayers seeing their after-tax income rise by 0.5%, while the top 20% saw their after-tax incomes rise by 4.9% and the top 1% saw their income rise by 6.6%, a distribution that critics highlight benefits wealthier taxpayers.[19] While comparative estimates of the distributional impact of the Reid and Hatch proposals are currently unavailable, the Reid proposal may reduce some of the gains in after-tax income for upper income taxpayers that resulted from the Bush tax cuts and which would continue under the Hatch proposal.[20]

The distributional impact of the Bush tax cuts—and hence the impact of a full extension as proposed by Senator Hatch—may be relevant to policy makers if they are concerned with growing income inequality in the United States.[21] A recent CBO report highlighted that while the main driver of increasing after-tax income inequality was the increasing concentration of *pre-tax income* among the wealthiest Americans, government transfers and federal tax policy also contributed to the growth of after-tax income inequality.[22] As the CBO report indicated, the equalizing impact of taxes depends on their progressivity,[23] with increasing progressivity reducing income inequality (holding the size of tax receipts constant).[24] The Bush tax cuts overall reduced the progressivity of federal income taxes[25] and hence were a factor in increases in income inequality in the United States, according to CBO. In this case, allowing the Bush tax cuts to expire for upper income earners would result in a more progressive tax code in comparison to an extension for all taxpayers.

End Notes

[1] Conceptually S. 3413 is similar to S. 3401, but includes an additional provision extending section 179 expensing for one year. Similarly, S. 3412 is similar to S. 3393, but does not address the estate tax.

[2] Michael Beller, "Senate Democrats Drop Estate Tax Language From 2001, 2003 Tax Cut Bill," *Tax Notes Today*, July 20, 2012, 2012 TNT 140-1.

[3] Other laws enacted during the Bush Administration accelerated the implementation of certain provisions of EGTRRA and JGTRRA or modified provisions in these bills, including the Working Families Tax Relief Act of 2004 (WFTRA; P.L. 108-311), The Tax Increase Prevention and Reconciliation Act of 2005 (TIPRA; P.L. 109-222) and the Emergency Economic Stabilization Act of 2008 (EESA; P.L. 110-343).

[4] For more information on the estate tax, see CRS Report 95-444, *A History of Federal Estate, Gift, and Generation-Skipping Taxes*, by John R. Luckey and CRS Report RL30600, *Estate and Gift Taxes: Economic Issues*, by Donald J. Marples and Jane G. Gravelle.

[5] The federal estate and gift taxes are unified. This means that these taxes have the same rate structure. The federal gift tax is imposed on lifetime gifts of property. For more information the relationship between the estate and gift taxes, see CRS Report 95-416, *Federal Estate, Gift, and Generation-Skipping Taxes: A Description of Current Law*, by John R. Luckey.

[6] For more information on the AMT, see CRS Report RL30149, *The Alternative Minimum Tax for Individuals*, by Steven Maguire.

[7] According to the legislative language, these thresholds will be indexed for inflation occurring since 2009.

[8] Joint Committee on Taxation, *Estimated Revenue Effects of the "Middle Class Tax Cut Act"*, July 19, 2012, #12-2- 112 R3 and Joint Committee on Taxation, *Estimated Revenue Effects of a Possible Modification to the "Tax Relief Act of 2012,"* July 18, 2012, #12-2-116.

[9] Joint Committee on Taxation, *Estimated Revenue Effects of HR.8, the "Job Protection and Recession Prevention Act of 2012,"* July 24, 2012, JCX-64-12.

[10] A more detailed overview of the policy debate, including on provisions not addressed in this paper, like the AMT, can be found in CRS Report R42485, *An Overview of Tax Provisions Expiring in 2012*, by Margot L. Crandall-Hollick.

[11] For more information on the economic impact of capital gains taxation, including a distribution analysis of beneficiaries of lower capital gains rates, see CRS Report R40411, *The Economic Effects of Capital Gains Taxation*, by Thomas L. Hungerford.

[12] In an analysis of the budgetary cost of the Bush tax cuts, CBO stated: "The policies [Bush tax cuts] undoubtedly exerted at least some influence on the economy...Those economic feedbacks on today's budget, however, are likely to be modest." For more information, see Congressional Budget Office, *Letter to the Honorable John M. Spratt, Jr.*, July 20, 2007, http://www.cbo.gov/sites/default/files/cbofiles/ftpdocs/83xx/doc8337/07-20-egtrra-jgtrra_and_deficits.pdf.

[13] Lowering marginal tax rates would theoretically increase the amount taxpayers work and so would theoretically increase their income (all else being equal). The sensitivity of income to changes in marginal tax rates is referred to as elasticity. An elasticity less than one implies that changes in taxpayers' income were proportionally less than the changes in the tax rate, while an elasticity greater than one implies that income gains are proportionally larger than the tax cut. A recent review of other studies found that the elasticity of income to tax rate changes was between 0.12 to 0.40. Since the resulting increase in income is proportionally smaller than the cut in marginal rates, government revenues will fall as a result of the cut. See Emmanuel Saez, Joel Slemrod, and Seth Giertz, "The Elasticity of Taxable Income with Respect to Marginal Tax Rates: A Critical Review," *Journal of Economic Literature*, vol. 50, no. 1 (2012), pp. 42. Similarly, CBO found that a 10% tax rate cut would offset between 5%-32% of the cost of cut in terms of revenue losses over the second 5 years of a year budgetary window. For more information, see Congressional Budget Office, *Analyzing the Economic and Budgetary Effects of a 10 Percent Cut in Income Tax Rates*, Economic and Budget Issue Brief, December 1, 2005, http://www.cbo.gov/sites/default/files/cbofiles/ftpdocs/69xx/doc6908/12-01- 10percenttaxcut.pdf. In so far as tax cuts are deficit-financed, they may actually negatively impact growth. For example, the Joint Committee on Taxation, in modeling the economic effects of reducing individual and corporate tax rates, found that "Growth eventually become(s) negative without offsetting fiscal policy...because accumulating Federal government debt crowds out private investment." Joint Committee on

Taxation, *Macroeconomic Analysis of Various Proposals to Provide $500 Billion in Tax Relief*, JCX-4-05, March 1, 2005, p. 2.

[14] See Table 1, CBO, Policies for Increasing Economic Growth and Employment in 2012 and 2013, November 2011, http://www.cbo.gov/publication/42717. Of the policies examined, tax cuts were one of the least stimulative.

[15] Mark Zandi, chief economist at Moody's Analytics, testified to the Joint Economic Committee that the scheduled spending cuts included in the Budget Control Act which go into effect in 2013 and combined expiration of extended unemployment insurance benefits, the payroll tax cuts, and the Bush tax cuts in 2013 will reduce real GDP growth by nearly 3 percentage points in 2013. See http://jec.senate.gov/public//index.cfm?a=Files.Serve& File_id=df 8f2728-94fa4339-992a-a9b8d2505fc2.

[16] CBO, *Change in CBO's Baseline Projection of the Surplus Since January 2001*, May 12, 2011, http://www.cbo.gov/ sites/default/files/cbofiles/ftpdocs/121xx/doc12187/changes baseline projections.pdf.

[17] Joint Committee on Taxation, *Estimated Budget Effects of the "Tax Relief Unemployment Insurance Reauthorization and Job Creation Act of 2010", Scheduled for Consideration by the United States Senate*, December 10, 2010, JCX-54- 10.

[18] Joint Committee on Taxation, *Estimated Revenue Effects of the "Middle Class Tax Cut Act"*, July 19, 2012, #12-2- 112 R3 and Joint Committee on Taxation, *Estimated Revenue Effects of a Possible Modification to the "Tax Relief Act of 2012"*, July 18, 2012, #12-2-116.

[19] Tax Policy Center. These estimates include the impact of the AMT-patch and the 2008 EESA recovery payments. Table T10-0232.

[20] However certain provisions of the Bush tax cuts which tend to benefit upper income taxpayers like the preferential tax rates on capital gains and dividends do not expire under the Reid proposal. Instead of the marginal tax rates for both dividend and capita gains rise to 20% for upper income taxpayers (if the Bush tax cuts expired, dividend would be taxed as ordinary income). For more information on the distributional impact of the preferential capital gains tax rates can be found in CRS Report R40411, *The Economic Effects of Capital Gains Taxation*, by Thomas L. Hungerford.

[21] For example see, Emmanuel Saez, "Striking It Richer: The Evolution of Top Income in the United States (Updated with 2009 and 2010 estimates)," March 2, 2012, http://emlab.berkeley.edu/~saez/saez-UStopincomes-2010.pdf. In addition, see CRS Report R42400, *The U.S. Income Distribution and Mobility: Trends and International Comparisons*, by Linda Levine.

[22] CBO, *Trends in the Distribution of Household Income Between 1979 and 2007*, October. 2011.

[23] The current federal income tax is progressive meaning that taxes as a share of income increases as income levels of increase.

[24] CBO, *Trends in the Distribution of Household Income Between 1979 and 2007*, October. 2011, p. 20.

[25] CBO, *Trends in the Distribution of Household Income Between 1979 and 2007*, October 2011, p. 27.

INDEX

D

E

F

G

R

S

T

U

V

W

Y